GARDENING TIPS
FROM THE
NATIONAL TRUST

THE NATIONAL TRUST

Illustrations by: Sophie Allington, Norman Charlton, Brian Delf, John Dyke, Brin Edwards, Elizabeth Jane Lloyd, Claude Page, David Peacock, Ian Penney, Eric Thomas, Soun Vannithone

Front cover: Hostas and bluebells.
National Trust Photographic Library/Andrew Lawson

British Library Cataloguing-in-Publication Data
A catalogue record for this book is available from the British Library

Published in Great Britain by
The National Trust (Enterprises) Ltd,
36 Queen Anne's Gate, London SW1H 9AS

Designed by Pardoe Blacker Ltd, Lingfield, Surrey
Phototypeset in Monotype Bembo, Series 270
by Southern Positives and Negatives (SPAN), Lingfield, Surrey
Printed in England by Clays Ltd, Bungay, Suffolk

Contents

JULY TO SEPTEMBER

OCTOBER TO DECEMBER

Preface

HAPPY IS THE MAN with the keen intellect and superhuman eagerness to reveal the innermost secrets of nature; happy is he who can grasp the causes and relationships of matter; who can walk in the footsteps of Newton as his companion. But happy too is the man who cares for his fields; who appreciates all the manifold riches of his garden; who has learnt the art of grafting trees that each may thrive in its favourite soil; and who knows which are the happiest in the rich mud and ooze of the pond; which rejoice on the rocky ridges; which shun the biting cold of the north wind; and which flower high up in the snowy wastes of Scythia. Do not scorn or grumble about this modest toil; it is shared by the greatest gardener of all. Do not look for Him only amid the stars of heaven; for it is in the ordinary things of life that you may find God.

Translation of the Latin text inscribed on the glass of the east window of the library at Montacute House in Somerset.

Translated by JONATHAN H. MUSGRAVE.

Introduction

EACH NATIONAL TRUST GARDEN is unique. Each is made up of a different mix of qualities and associations – historic, horticultural, artistic, personal and local. But common to all our gardens is the way that their character and impact are directly dependent on the standard of their upkeep. The quality of the gardening has a fundamental effect not only on their day-to-day appearance but also on their long-term conservation and development. Major operations – fellings, plantings, renewals – have an important part to play but every routine task has a cumulative effect.

The style of the gardener is instantly recognisable and, whatever the checks and balances may be, it is upon his or her skills and judgements that the garden depends. Just as in the theatre enjoyment is dependent both on the original script and the quality of the staging and performance, so much the same applies in gardens which have to be re-created from day to day and year to year. The quality of the original idea has to be constantly reinterpreted according to the modern constraints imposed by the National Trust's limited resources and the fact that our gardens are enjoyed by large numbers of visitors.

The reservoir of gardening expertise and fine judgement that exists among the gardeners employed by the Trust is unsurpassed. It is part of our job as Gardens Advisers to nurture, develop and spread this professionalism and ensure that it can be passed on from generation to generation. Opportunities are provided within the Trust for experienced gardeners to pool their expertise and for young gardeners to be trained under the guidance of an expert gardener.

This book aims to share more widely some of this knowledge and experience and our gardeners have responded generously with their time and know-how. You will soon discover, if you don't already know, that success in gardening comes largely as a result of consistent hard work and attention to detail. As well as horticultural skill, gardening at its best involves foresight, imagination, careful observation and sound aesthetic judgement based on the particular ideal of the garden in question, with its own history, planting, locality and, most important of all, the spirit and taste of those who originally created it.

In reflecting and perpetuating this diversity it is the style of gardening that counts most. While techniques need to be soundly based and practical, in gardening there are many ways of achieving a satisfactory result, depending on the location and the resources available. You will see that in the Trust these different methods are encouraged. Nothing would be worse than standard procedures being allowed to impose a monotonous conformity everywhere. Far from regularising its approach to gardens, the Trust promotes variety as much as possible through policy and practice, in the face of strong economic and other pressures to conform.

This diversity is carried through into this book. Apart from their arrangement, month by month, there is neither a regular pattern to the contributions, nor to the contributors. The aim is to stimulate the reader with ideas, encouragement and practical advice on a range of topics appropriate to the time of year. There is no attempt at comprehensive coverage of garden tasks and this is not the book to consult for a month by month list of garden tasks.

While many of the accounts and the tips can be applied directly to smaller private gardens, others will give an insight into the challenges faced in running historic gardens and into the characters who look after them. It would be difficult to find a group of people in any profession more deeply committed to their work than those in charge of the Trust's gardens.

JOHN SALES
Chief Gardens Adviser

Gardens and
the National Trust

THE NATIONAL TRUST is the largest conservation organisation in Britain, independent of government. Founded in 1895, it is a registered charity committed to preserving for the nation our finest countryside, coastline, historic buildings, landscape, parks and gardens in England, Wales and Northern Ireland.

The Trust now has 172 gardens in its care with 386 gardeners. Details of all these gardens may be found in the National Trust Annual Handbook, free to members and available to non-members from NT shops, properties and bookshops. It can also be purchased by post from the National Trust Head Office, 36 Queen Anne's Gate, London SW1H 9AS. Please send a cheque for £5.50 to cover the cost of the book, postage and packing. *The National Trust Gardens Handbook* is also a useful publication with details of Trust gardens, best times to visit, facilities available etc. This book costs £3.95 and is available from NT shops and bookshops or by mail order from The National Trust (Enterprises) Ltd, PO Box 101, Melksham, Wiltshire SN12 8EA (Tel. 0225 705676). Please send a cheque for £4.95 to cover postage and packing.

CAREERS IN GARDENING

IN 1989 the National Trust introduced a careership training in amenity horticulture for school leavers who wish to become gardeners. It is unique to the National Trust and combines location training with college tuition. For further details, send a stamped addressed envelope to The National Trust Careership Office, Lanhydrock, Bodmin, Cornwall PL30 4DE.

JANUARY
TO
MARCH

THE CONSERVATORY IN WINTER

John H. Ellis, Head Gardener

WALLINGTON · CAMBO · MORPETH · NORTHUMBERLAND

The conservatory at Wallington has a splendid display of plants all year round but every season is spectacular in the garden. The flowering shrubs produce a delightful display in late spring, the herbaceous borders are stunning in summer and there is outstanding autumn woodland colour.

The conservatory is an ideal link between the garden and the home and can enhance both, even in the depths of winter.

Heating the conservatory

The two most important factors in the conservatory during the winter months are heat and light. The first requires more thought and the equation of use, cost and enjoyment should be considered. If at all possible the conservatory should be kept at least frost-free. For each additional degree that a conservatory is heated, more and more plants can be accommodated and the environment becomes more comfortable for family and friends.

Light

The second factor – the quality of light – can be much improved simply by routine winter hygiene. It is very important to wash down the conservatory at least once a year. There are proprietary cleaners for glass but benches, walls and surfaces should all be washed down with diluted Jeyes fluid or a mild solution of bleach, then well rinsed. This not only allows maximum light penetration during the darkest time of the year – glass actually reduces light intensity rather than magnifying it – but also keeps in check a variety of pests, such as red spider mite and mealy bug. This chore is perhaps best done in the late autumn or early winter in order to enjoy the maximum benefit of your efforts.

TIPS

As with many things in life the more time and care you invest in your conservatory, the greater the enjoyment you gain. The incentive is there, for a well-stocked and staged conservatory can brighten up many a dark winter's day. Here are ten tips which will assist with that aim.

1. Avoid too much heat. Check the plants for water and general health daily if possible. Hot pipes can make your plants dry out very quickly even during the coldest weather. If plants are directly over the source of heat the leaves may be killed.

2. Watering. When watering look at each plant individually. This is particularly important when a wide variety of plants is being grown as they often dry out at different rates. Feel the compost for dryness or test the weight of the plant before watering. When you decide to water, apply enough to wet the pot ball thoroughly.

3. Arrangement. Staging (arranging) plants correctly is very important and when done tastefully gives a professional look. There are many styles but they all follow the same principle – grade the plants so that tall subjects are at the back, graduating to trailing plants at the front.
The density of plants can vary according to taste. Some people like to space the plants out well, so that each speci-

men is shown standing on its own. Some like plants to be so close that they hide the pots, while others allow just enough space to enjoy the full shape of each specimen. Keep in mind that if plants are too close together, air circulation will be poor and the plants may suffer.

4. Dead leaves. Remove dead or dying leaves as soon as they appear and never allow leaf litter to build up. Otherwise pests can continue their lifecycle and diseases like *Botrytis* (grey mould) can become a problem.

5. Putting plants outside. Many winter-flowering plants, such as *Justica rizzinii* (syn. *Jacobinia pauciflora*), *Hardenbergia violacea, Rhododendron* 'Fragrantissimum' and *Buddleja auriculata*, can be placed outside during the summer.

6. Ventilation. Ventilate when possible; fresh air is equally welcome in winter and, if common sense is used, this need not result in higher fuel bills. Opening the vents for a short period on a mild winter's day is often advantageous.

7. Pruning. Prune where appropriate at the correct time; this is often after flowering. In addition to standard benefits this allows some of the plant to be discarded, along with any pests and diseases it may be carrying. For the same reason, throw out any plants that are irretrievably past their best.

8. Bulbs. Do not forget bulbs. There is a wide variety available, many of them unusual. They are a good way of shortening the winter and enjoying an early spring.

9. Photographs. Keep a photographic record of the displays in the conservatory. This allows seasons and different years to be compared and will assist in making improvements.

10. Know your plants. Be intimate with your plants. Pick them up, wipe them over, give them a manicure. The best gardeners are observant and know their plants.

POT PLANTS AND CUT FLOWERS FOR THE HOUSE

Mary Digby, Assistant Head Gardener

CHARTWELL · WESTERHAM · KENT

Sir Winston and Lady Churchill planned the garden at Chartwell in a country-garden style with terraced lawns, ponds, flower beds and an orchard. The colour schemes are particularly attractive and there is a golden rose walk created in 1958 to commemorate their golden wedding.

At Chartwell we provide flowering pot plants and cut flowers for the nine months the house is open. We cultivate the same varieties that were grown when Sir Winston and Lady Churchill were alive, adhering to their colour preferences.

Varieties

The main pot plants are hyacinths, amaryllis, regal pelargoniums, fuchsias, tuberous begonias and, for November, Charm chrysanthemums. Cut flowers include forced and naturalised daffodils, sweet peas, roses and dahlias. We propagate everything ourselves by cuttings or seed, except for plants grown from bulbs or corms which we buy in each year.

Potting Compost

We mix our own compost using 7 parts loam, 3 parts peat, 2 parts Chichester grit plus a slow-release fertiliser like Osmocote. The loam is cut from a heap of layered inverted turves and manure which has been left for at least a year to rot down, then chopped and put through a coarse sieve before mixing.

Bulbs

Hyacinth bulbs are planted three to a pot in early November, placed outside, covered with 6in/15cm of soil, then lifted in February and brought into a cool greenhouse to flower in March. The daffodils are given the same treatment but are planted 50 bulbs to a wooden box.

The original amaryllis (*Hippeastrum*) was given to Sir Winston when he was ill by Princess Marina, Duchess of Kent, and he was so taken with it that he said he always wanted them at Chartwell. After flowering the plants are fed and watered regularly until the leaves start to die down. They are then put in a frame for the summer as a temperature of 70°F/21°C is needed for next year's flower buds to form. In October, when the foliage has died back, the pots are put on their sides under the greenhouse bench and left alone. When the buds begin to appear in spring the pots are stood up and watered. This is the time to repot them, teasing out all the dead roots and soil, making sure the pot is not too large and leaving the top half of the bulb uncovered.

Pelargoniums

In early September, cuttings of regal pelargoniums are taken from stock plants lined out in the garden. Three cuttings are potted in a 3in/7.5cm pot and placed on the greenhouse bench. When rooted, one cutting is removed from each pot. They are grown at a temperature of 50°F/10°C throughout the winter and potted on twice to flower in April/May. The final pot size for all plants is 6in/15cm in diameter as they fit well into the white ceramic cache-pôts used in the house.

Fuchsias

Fuchsia cuttings are taken in October, rooted in the propagation frame in the greenhouse in a 50:50 mixture of peat and grit, potted up singly in 3in/7.5cm pots and potted on as necessary. They are stopped, or pinched out, several times to make bushy plants and some of the more pendulous varieties are grown on a short leg or stem. Flowering occurs six weeks after the final stopping. Fuchsias do not like the darkish rooms of Chartwell so need changing frequently.

Sweet peas

Sweet peas are sown in pots in November, placed in a cold frame to overwinter, then stopped in late January to encourage strong basal growths, which are reduced to one shoot per plant when planted out in April. They are trained up bamboo canes tied to supporting wires and side-shoots and tendrils are removed to get long, straight flower stalks. Flowering should be from June to September in a good season and the plants will have to be laid in August when they reach the top of their canes. This entails releasing them from their canes, laying their stems along the ground and tying them up to canes about 3ft/0.9m away.

Dahlias

Dahlias usually flower until the end of October, as Chartwell escapes early frosts because the garden is on a slope. The tubers are stored in the basement of the frost-free house in winter. They should be left loose in a box or on a dry floor and checked regularly to ensure no damp has reached them. They should be brought into growth in frames before planting in the garden the following spring. (*See also* DEALING WITH DAHLIAS, *p.106*.)

Other plants grown for cutting include tulips, De Caen Anemones, Dutch and Spanish Iris, gladioli, Canterbury Bells, Sweet Williams, aquilegia, *Alstroemeria* Ligtu Hybrids, asters, larkspur, cosmos and lavatera.

TIPS

1. Petunias make good pot plants if one colour is used rather than mixed seed. Choose strongly-scented varieties, particularly the violet-blue Multiflora types which usually have good scent. Prick out 3 seedlings into a 3in/7.5cm pot and pot on when necessary. If cut back after the first flush of flowers the plants will flower again.

2. *Cosmos* Sensation Mixed is an excellent annual for picking as it flowers profusely all summer. The plants do need supporting, however, as they can reach 4ft/1.2m in height.

AFTER THE STORM

George Fillis, Head Gardener

EMMETTS GARDEN · IDE HILL · SEVENOAKS · KENT

The style of the influential Victorian gardener William Robinson can be seen in this 5-acre shrub garden which is said to be the highest in Kent. Exotic species are underplanted with naturalised bulbs, there is an Italianate rose garden and a restored rock garden.

After the great storm on 16 October 1987, Emmetts Garden had changed, not only in appearance but also in climate. Once sheltered by high woodland, it is now very exposed to high winds and strong sunlight and the replanting has had to be carefully considered.

Compost

In January, weather permitting, we plant new shrubs and trees and, because the ground is free-draining, we incorporate plenty of compost into the planting hole to help retain moisture. Our compost contains well-rotted horse manure, grass cuttings and leaves, and is stacked for two years. As well as being used for planting it is also used for mulching – again to help retain moisture and to suppress weed growth, therefore saving many hours of weeding during the summer.

Mulching materials

There are many types of material that can be used for mulching, including composts such as mushroom compost. This contains lime so must not be used around lime-hating plants. Wood chips are a good mulch but need to be stacked for a year because if used fresh they will take nitrogen from the soil. Forest bark is good but expensive, while coconut fibre is now recommended as a peat substitute. All of these make good mulches and, if applied while the soil is wet, will help retain moisture for the summer, as well as suppress weed growth.

Trees to choose

Replacing the shelter-belt/wind-break for the garden is slow as most of the land slopes away from the gardens so the trees have to grow tall to be effective. Quick-growing trees have been planted to help. We have used conifers, such as Scots Pine (*Pinus sylvestris*) and Monterey Pine (*Pinus radiata*), and broad-leaved trees, such as Italian Alder (*Alnus cordata*), as well as our native oak (*Quercus robur*), Red Oak (*Quercus rubra*) and beech (*Fagus sylvatica*) for the longer term. These are then underplanted with Field Maple (*Acer campestre*), hazel (*Corylus avellana*) and holly (*Ilex aquifolium*).

While it is unlikely that a storm as fierce as the 1987 hurricane will occur again, there are always winter winds which cause damage and these suggestions may prove useful, whatever the size of your garden.

TIP

Whatever the size of your garden, shelter is important. Check fences each year; winter winds whistling through a few missing slats can cause a surprising amount of damage.

PRUNING AND TRAINING CLIMBERS

Sarah Cook, Head Gardener

SISSINGHURST GARDEN · NR CRANBROOK · KENT

In 1930 Vita Sackville-West and Harold Nicolson began to create their famous garden at Sissinghurst Castle. Dividing the space into a series of compartments, they conjured up inspired and informal arrangements of plants and a brilliant variety of colour and design. Particularly famous is the White Garden, with its cascades of white flowers and grey foliage in summer.

The walls of the ruined Elizabethan mansion which are such a feature of this garden, are covered with a wide variety of climbing plants. Many climbers are best pruned during the winter months, and certainly all the work described below can be carried out at any time between November and mid-March. Avoid very frosty conditions, and if you choose a sunny day, the job will be much more pleasant.

Time to prune

At Sissinghurst we do nearly all the training and pruning of wall shrubs in the winter, thus avoiding trampling the plantings at the foot of the wall. There are two exceptions; tender plants (eg *Solanum* and *Fremontodendron*) are best pruned and tied in late March; and wisteria, *Chaenomeles* and early flowering clematis species should be pruned in summer.

Objectives

There are five main objectives to be achieved.

(1) The means of attachment to the wall (wires, nails, trellises etc) must be secure. Replace as necessary. Tie the main structure of the climber firmly to the supports and ensure these ties will last until the following year.

(2) The plant must be kept within the allotted space, so cut out large limbs if necessary. Also space the limbs evenly over the allotted space, retying where necessary to encourage a well-shaped plant.

(3) The desired amount of new healthy growth must be encouraged again, ruthlessly if need be.

(4) The correct balance between new growth and flowers must be maintained, with good quality blooms the principal aim.

(5) The plants should be kept away from gutters and windows; steer clear of telephone wires and television aerials with the secateurs.

To achieve these objectives with different plants requires a variety of treatments. For clarity I have divided the plants into five categories and most wall plants fit into one of them.

Self-clingers

Eg *Hydrangea anomala* subsp. *petiolaris, Pileostegia viburnoides*
Deadhead; reduce a proportion of the longest growths to a bud about 9in/23cm from the wall.

Summer-flowering shrubs

Eg *Viburnum, Pyracantha, Garrya*
These do not usually need detailed pruning. Make a few large cuts (not necessarily every year) rather than lots of small ones. Leave them looking as natural as possible. Cut out some old branches to prevent the shrub becoming overcrowded and to encourage some new growth which can be tied in to replace old branches, thus keeping the shrub young.

Vines

These should be pruned before mid-January. Cut all new growth to a bud within 2in/5cm of the framework. In the first 3–5 years after replanting new growths should be cut to 18–24in/45–60cm and fanned out to make a permanent framework.

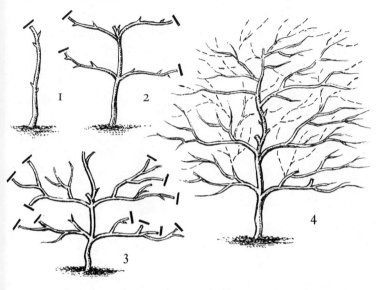

FIGS.1, 2 *and* 3 *indicate where to make cuts to build up a permanent framework on vines.* FIG.4 *shows the permanent structure of the vine with surplus new growth removed each year.*

Climbing roses

It is most important to maintain a balance between growth and flowers. Making cuts near the base of a shoot will stimulate new shoots rather than flowers. During the first few years cut all growth by two-thirds to make a strong framework. Mature climbers need to have some of the oldest and weakest branches cut out, some to ground level if possible, some to a strong branch part way up. For new shoots, reduce some of the strongest by over half and these will make more new shoots for the framework; for

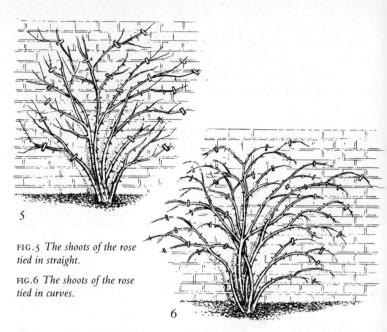

FIG. 5 *The shoots of the rose tied in straight.*

FIG. 6 *The shoots of the rose tied in curves.*

the rest cut off less than one-third and tie in so that these will produce flowers and more new shoots. Weak new shoots should be reduced to 2–6 buds to produce flowers (for *very* weak shoots leave 2 buds, more for stronger shoots). Tie in straight or curved to taste (*see figs. 5 and 6*).

Clematis

For early, large flowered hybrids, eg 'Nelly Moser', reduce shoots to a strong pair of buds, removing dead and weak growth. For late flowerers, eg *C. viticella*, cut back shoots to a pair of buds just above ground level.

TIP

Check the ground you will be standing on before you start pruning. If there are interesting looking seedlings, carefully transplant them somewhere safer or pot them up.

PRUNING SHRUBS

Philip Rollinson, Head Gardener

SALTRAM HOUSE · PLYMPTON · PLYMOUTH · DEVON

Saltram's is a late eighteenth-century garden of 20 acres altered to its present design in the nineteenth century. Magnolias, camellias and narcissi are glorious features in spring and there are delightful walks bordered by specimen trees and shrubs. Cyclamen hederifolium *and outstanding leaf colour provide spectacular autumnal effects.*

February is considered to be the last month of winter or the first month of spring depending on weather and locality. After a mild winter, much pruning, feeding and mulching can be done during this month, but if there is any doubt then leave it until mid–March.

Which shrubs to prune?

Shrubs that need pruning now are those that flower on the current season's growth, that is they bloom in the second half of the summer or through the winter. With Winter Jasmine (*Jasminum nudiflorum*), for example, aim to keep as much of the new green growth as possible, while cutting right out some of the old pale brown stems. The old wood that is left can be supported, allowing the strong new growth that bears next year's flowers to flourish gracefully.

If left unpruned these deciduous shrubs will become reduced in vigour and have smaller and poorer flowers. The removal of a large amount of wood means the energy of the shrubs goes to fewer shoots and flowers which are then larger and of better quality.

23

All shoots, therefore, can be cut back hard to within 2–3 buds of ground level. Hard pruning delays flowering, but if you wish to extend the flowering period cut half the shoots back to 2–3 buds and the remainder to a half or third of their length.

Tools for the job
Make sure you have the right tools for the job beforehand:

☐ sharp secateurs which are correctly set (blunt or badly set secateurs can result in tears and bruising which can lead to die back and/or infection – especially relevant to roses)
☐ pruning lopper for thick wood
☐ a narrow-bladed saw or a bow saw
☐ strong leather gloves.

Method
As with all pruning, carry out the basic tasks first:

☐ remove dead, damaged or diseased wood and weak or straggly growth
☐ remove any suckers and crossing or rubbing branches
☐ try to retain an open framework by cutting back some of the main stems to the base.

Some deciduous shrubs that should be pruned now include: *Buddleja davidii*; *Caryopteris* × *clandonensis*; deciduous *Ceanothus* eg 'Gloire de Versailles'; *Ceratostigma*; hardy fuchsias; *Hydrangea paniculata*; *Indigofera*; *Perovskia*; *Prunus triloba*; *Romneya*; *Spiraea douglasii* and *S. japonica*.

Coppicing
Shrubby plants grown for their decorative winter bark should be coppiced now, ie cut hard back. Coppicing stimulates the growth of new, vigorous stems with especially strong colour. Cut all stems to 2–3in/5–7.5cm from the base. Apply fertiliser and mulch. This group of shrubs includes: dogwoods eg *Cornus alba* and *C. stolonifera*; *Salix* spp.; *Rubus cockburnianus* (Ornamental Bramble); *Cotinus coggygria*; *Corylus maxima* 'Purpurea' (Purple Filbert) and *Sambucus* (golden-leaved and purple-leaved forms). If you require

bigger shrubs or a looser effect, prune on a two-year cycle, removing the two-year-old stems each year but leaving the one-year-old ones. Hard pruning of *Corylus* and *Sambucus* generally results in larger leaves.

Wall shrubs

Wall shrubs that are deciduous and flower on the current season's growth should be cut hard back to the framework as previously described, eg *Ceanothus*. Some young stems may be left unpruned apart from a light tipping.

Hydrangeas

These fall into three groups for pruning purposes:

- [ ] those that flower on current season's growth, eg *H. paniculata*. Cut hard back to a framework near ground level.
- [ ] those that flower on one-year-old wood, eg the mop-heads and lacecaps such as *H. macrophylla*. Pruning can be delayed as the old flowerheads give protection to overwintering flowerbuds. Cut out some of the older wood to the base and remove weak shoots. The other stems can then be shortened to a strong pair of buds.
- [ ] a third group containing other species, such as *H. aspera*, needs only minimal pruning now.

Feeding and mulching

After pruning, apply a base dressing of general fertiliser at 120gsm (a good handful). Now is a good time to mulch around your shrubs with leaf compost, shredded bark or wood chippings.

TIP

For shrubs with *alternate* buds prune to just above a bud or shoot using a clean, angled cut. The lowest point of the cut should be opposite the base of the bud. For shrubs with *opposite* shoots prune to just above a strong pair of buds or shoots using a clean, straight cut.

CITRUS FRUIT IN POTS AND TUBS

Michael Marshall, Head Gardener

DUNSTER CASTLE · DUNSTER · NR MINEHEAD · SOMERSET

The wooded garden at Dunster Castle extends over 17 acres, with southeast slopes and terraces that are ideal for sun-loving plants. Camellias and magnolias flourish and there is a fine citrus collection. Dunster is home to the National Collection of Arbutus.

Although mainly grown in warm countries with a Mediterranean-type climate, with a little care many species of citrus can be cultivated in Britain. The main requirements are frost-free conditions, correct watering and feeding, as much sunshine as possible and correct planting.

Choosing the right species

Many species can be grown in cool climates and still produce prolific amounts of fruit. Kumquats (*Fortunella japonica* and *F. margarita*) and the Myrtle-leaf Orange (*Citrus aurantium* var. *myrtifolia*), Satsuma and Mandarin Oranges (*C. reticulata*), Seville Orange (*C. aurantium*), Pummelo or Shaddock (*C. maxima*, syn. *C. grandis*) are just a few. Perhaps the easiest citrus to cultivate is the lemon. At Dunster Castle, on the south-facing terrace, there is a lemon tree thought to be well over 100 years old. It produces fruit throughout the year and it is possible to have ripe fruit, unripe fruit and flowers on the tree at the same time.

Sweet orange and grapefruit can also be cultivated successfully, but these need many hours of sunshine to produce edible fruit and they are also less hardy than the lemon. Citrus are not deciduous and only lose a few leaves at a time. They continue growing most of the year. However, in the winter, when the plants are kept at a temperature of no less than 45–50°F/7–10°C, watering is reduced to a minimum and feeding is stopped to enforce a pause in growth. Flowers can still be observed in mid-winter and the fruit sets in both spring and summer, and can hang on the tree for a full year before ripening.

Cultivation

Cultivation can start with young plants or pips in February and early March. Most citrus pips are viable and can be germinated in a temperature of 65–75°F/18–24°C. It is also possible to take stem cuttings; those taken from *Citrus limon* in August and September can produce fruit in 2–3 years if kept over winter in a warm greenhouse. The period of time it takes for a tree to reach fruiting size can vary from 5–10 years.

Potting

Citrus will tolerate most types of soil, but a well-draining potting compost, such as John Innes No.3, with added sand, is a good medium. It is very important to plant the tree at the correct depth in the soil. Citrus have very thin bark which makes them suscep-tible to disease if the top of the root ball is too far below the soil line. Pot at the same depth each time the plant is repotted. Good drainage to avoid waterlogging is essential; place broken crocks in the bottom of the pot and fill gradually with compost. Firm well at intervals until the soil is 1in/2.5cm from the top. From this point careful watering is essential. Do not over-water. Pot-bound trees can be re-potted at any time of the year, but early spring is considered best because this gives the plant the whole summer to make new roots and establish itself before the cold of winter.

Position

In May, when the fear of frost has passed, the pots or tubs may be put outside. Choose a south-facing wall, away from wind, preferably on a paved or slabbed area. Stand the trees about two or three feet (just under a metre) from the wall so that the sun will be reflected from two surfaces to give maximum heat and light.

Feeding

Feed the plant every 7–10 days with a well-balanced fertiliser. Whether applied systemically or directly to the soil, the main element citrus plants require is nitrogen.

Orange and lemon trees are a wonderful addition to any garden and as house plants they can look superb. Even without fruit the colour and beauty of the plant can give great pleasure for many years.

TIP
To avoid chlorosis, yellowing of the leaf, water only with *rainwater*, not tap water.

LAWN MAINTENANCE

Richard Ayres, Head Gardener

ANGLESEY ABBEY · LODE · CAMBRIDGESHIRE

The 100-acre garden created in 1926 is an imposing blend of the formal seventeenth-century French style and eighteenth-century natural land-scaping. As well as wide, grassy walks and avenues, there is a dahlia garden, a hyacinth garden, a curved herbaceous border and an impressive collection of statuary.

Most of us tend to forget our lawns during the winter months, using them just for access to our vegetable plots or for exercising our pets. As soon as the sun comes out and the days get warmer we realise that the grass has started to grow and the lawn requires attention.

Preparation for the first cut

A healthy lawn requires some maintenance during the winter months. Most benefit from a good sweep with a besom broom two or three times during the winter to remove leaves and rubbish and to make the area look tidy.

Before giving the lawn its first cut, make sure all leaves and sticks are removed and that there are no stones on the lawn. Stones play havoc with the cutting mechanism of a cylinder mower. If you are not sure that all the small loose stones have been removed, run the mower over the lawn with the cutting cylinder raised up by bearing on the handles of the mower, so letting the back roller roll in the small stones.

Check that the cutting cylinder is not set too low before starting to mow, since it is a false belief that the shorter you cut the grass, the better your lawn will be. For a healthy lawn the cutting mechanism of the mower requires setting at about ½in/1cm off the ground. Frequent mowing is the answer to a good lawn, with regular cuts in as many directions as possible.

Feeding

Feeding is an important part of any lawn care programme. There are many types of fertiliser on the market that can be used and most of them are good when properly applied. They range from non-organic granular fertiliser to organic fertiliser and liquid feed. Choose fertilisers carefully taking into account the following:

- be careful when using non-organic fertiliser in dry weather, as it has a tendency to scorch the grass when the sun comes out. It is advisable to water in the fertiliser. A good maxim when using non-organic fertiliser is a little and often is better than a lot all at once.
- organic fertiliser and liquid feed can be used in dry spells, although organic fertiliser will require some moisture to help release nutrients.
- apply fertiliser to your lawn from April onwards, at least three times during the spring and summer, then another application of autumn fertiliser in late September.

Weedkilling

A selective lawn weedkiller is best used in spring after the weather has warmed up a bit and the grass is growing vigorously. Read the manufacturer's instructions carefully before use and follow them to the letter.

Spraying on a small lawn can be done successfully with a watering can fitted with a fine rose. If you are spraying your lawn in this way, mark out the area with either canes or string so that you do not miss any areas or go over parts of the lawn twice. Calibrate the amount of chemical you require per watering-can full. Half-fill the watering can with clean water, add the chemical, then top up with water. Mix well.

Make sure you are wearing gloves and Wellington boots. Take great care around the edges of the flower beds as it is better to miss a small area than to do irreparable damage to your plants. Pick a calm dry day to apply your lawn weedkiller. After you have finished, keep off the lawn for the rest of the day and make sure that none of your pets strays onto the lawn either. Remember that your watering can and rose will require thorough washing before you use it again for watering your garden plants.

Moss

Most lawns have moss to some degree. If part of your lawn is in the shade most of the day, moss could be a problem since it thrives in shady damp areas. Moss killers and feeding will help but moss has a habit of coming back when the conditions are ideal. Mowing the lawn too close to the ground with either a cylinder or rotary mower will also encourage moss. Again, moss killers will help, but raising the height of your blade will assist in keeping moss at bay. If your soil is poor or not very well drained or the lawn has not been fed for some years, moss will be encouraged to grow. Appropriate nutrients will help if poor soil is the major contributing factor to your moss problem.

Maintenance

Scarifying the lawn with a wire rake and spiking with a garden fork will encourage new growth in your grass and regular feeding will help to keep the lawn in good heart. A vital part of most gardens, lawns enhance the plants and give shape to the area. They are the best natural ground cover and require considerable attention in order to look their best.

TIP

Mow your lawn when it looks fine rather than when it begins to look a bit ragged. It will continue to look good and if you keep the edges well trimmed, they will provide the icing on the cake!

PRUNING ROSES

David Stone, Head Gardener

MOTTISFONT ABBEY GARDEN · NR ROMSEY · HAMPSHIRE

The 21-acre landscape garden which surrounds Mottisfont Abbey has a magnificent collection of trees, and also features work by Norah Lindsay and Geoffrey Jellicoe. The Rose Garden, laid out by the National Trust's second Gardens Adviser Graham Stuart Thomas in the walled kitchen garden in the 1970s and 1980s, holds the National Collection of Old (pre-1900) Roses.

There are no secrets to successful pruning. Sharp secateurs, strong gloves and an understanding of 'why' as well as 'when' and 'how' are all that you require.

When?

Early March is an excellent time to prune repeat flowering roses such as Hybrid Teas (large flowered), Floribundas (cluster flowered) and most modern shrubs and climbing varieties. For comfort's sake, choose a mild, dry day if possible, simply to make the work easier for yourself!

Why?

Roses will survive with the minimum of attention, but if they are to thrive a certain amount of careful pruning must be undertaken. Basically, we prune to: develop shape; control size; maintain vigour; encourage flowering and keep the plant healthy.

A well-shaped rose bush is an adornment to any garden, even in March! Maintain a balanced and open-branched structure by pruning main stems to an outward-facing bud, and completely removing any dead or entangling stems at, or near, ground level.

A tall rose cannot be kept short by hard pruning! However, careful attention at the right time can help to contain strong growing varieties to manageable proportions.

How?

Most repeat flowering roses can be divided into three pruning groups:

BUSH (HYBRID TEAS AND FLORIBUNDAS)

New plants should be pruned back hard to within 4–6in/10–15cm of the ground to encourage the formation of new, strong branches from near the plant's base (*see fig.1*). In subsequent years, prune away all weak or ageing wood before reducing the remaining stems by approximately one-half to two-thirds of their length (*see fig.2*). Strong growers, such as the ever popular 'Peace' (HT) and 'Iceberg' (Floribunda), can be pruned less severely. As a general rule, prune lightly for quantity of bloom, prune hard for quality of bloom!

FIG.1

FIG.2

CLIMBING ROSES

With new plants, the emphasis should be on training new shoots to cover the supporting wall or trellis. Shorter side shoots, which may have flowered the previous summer, are best pruned back to within a bud or two of the main stem. As the plants develop, they may become 'leggy', with flowers held above eye level. To encourage the formation of fresh young shoots from ground level, prune away completely the occasional older stem. If such stems are thicker than ½in/12mm, then long-handled pruners, or a small sharp saw, will be necessary to cope with these thicknesses. (*See also* PRUNING AND TRAINING CLIMBERS, *p.19*.)

MODERN SHRUB ROSES

This wide and varied group of mainly repeat flowering varieties includes the new 'English Roses' such as 'Graham Thomas', and the ever popular 'Ballerina'. In general, it may not be necessary to do more than tip back the leading shoots of established plants, but I prefer to reduce all new stems by approximately one-third of their length. According to the habit of growth, some thinning of stems may be required in order to avoid overcrowding, and hard pruning of older stems may from time to time prove necessary in order to encourage further new growth. Most shrub roses are best left to form largish specimens, although there are many excellent varieties available for the smaller garden.

TIPS

1. In July, thin out the oldest stems from once-flowering varieties of rambler and shrub roses as soon as blooms have faded.

2. In October, to avoid damage from strong autumnal winds, tie in the loose shoots and branches of climbing roses, and check the stem ties of standard roses.

3. In November or December, when planting new roses, incorporate two good handfuls of sterilised bonemeal into each planting hole. This should provide enough nutrients for the first season of growth.

STAKING HERBACEOUS BORDERS

Owen Sayer, Head Gardener

BLICKLING HALL · BLICKLING · NORWICH · NORFOLK

The delightful garden that surrounds the Jacobean mansion has several special features, including a Victorian sunken garden remodelled by Norah Lindsay in the 1930s with four parterre beds filled with colourful herbaceous flowers, yew topiary and a seventeenth-century fountain. Hidden in the northern wilderness is a secret garden with a summerhouse, sundial and scented plants.

Throughout the month of March herbaceous plants start to come alive in all National Trust gardens, so many gardeners begin to think about staking.

Pea sticks

Here at Blickling Hall in Norfolk, we use 'pea sticks' – hazelnut branches cut from our own woods in February while the trees are still dormant. Cut to lengths of approximately 8ft/2.4m, these branches are then cut down into three sizes: tips of branches for use with smaller plants, side branches for moderate height plants and the main branch for staking large plants (*see p.36*).

At Blickling staking takes place as soon as plants shoot, so that the plants grow through the pea sticks. This method provides support and helps protect young plants from rabbits. The pea sticks may look untidy to begin with but in a normal growing season the plants will cover the sticks in no time. However, in some dry seasons plants do not reach their normal height, so we have found it necessary to cut off sticks that were still showing.

Single stem plants

There are some plants, such as yuccas and verbascum, that have a single stem that cannot be supported by pea sticks. For these we use a short hazel stake pushed well into the ground, to give good

support at the base of the plant. The stake is then hidden by the lower foliage.

We find that hazel pea sticks only last for one season. Lime can be used but because it is a soft wood does not give good support. We use birch when we are short of hazel, but as it is compact, more stakes per plant are needed. Dead yew makes an excellent support and lasts up to three years, but it is hard to come by.

Hazelnut branches cut down to make pea sticks of three different sizes.

Alternatives to early staking

Although this approach to staking is used at Blickling Hall, other gardeners throughout the National Trust employ different methods. A method which results in the plant covering the stakes very quickly is to work stakes into the borders at the last possible moment, just before the plants flop over. The branches will still work themselves among the young shoots. Some gardeners break or bend over the tips of brushwood stakes, to make a top to the encircling brushwood cage through which the plants grow.

TIP
When the pea sticks have been made up into bundles, place a heavy board on top and the sprays will be flattened.

WATERSIDE PLANTING

Peter Hall, Head Gardener

DUNHAM MASSEY · ALTRINCHAM · CHESHIRE

This 20-acre informal garden was recreated by the National Trust in the 1970s with the help of a few existing records. In the past 20 years the Trust has replanted mixed borders and a wide range of shrubs and herbaceous borders and added waterside, courtyard and woodland plantings.

There is no doubt that work carried out on the water garden in March determines its success for the rest of the year. Whether through choice, design or accident you may have an area of wet ground you hope to enjoy throughout spring, summer and autumn with the minimum effort. It must look informal, watery and lush and yet, because of the wet conditions, once planted the site can be very difficult to work on. Compaction is the worst enemy on wet soil, and weeds germinate and grow with equal if not greater vigour than our chosen plants. The hoe is of no use in damp conditions, so we are restricted to hand-weeding or herbicides.

March is the month to put into practice measures that will, through some small effort now, guarantee relatively trouble-free water gardening throughout the rest of the season.

Early March

Begin by tidying the area. Choose a hard frosty day for this job and you will cause less compaction. I prefer to leave dead stems and

37

leaves in place throughout the winter to provide protection for plant crowns and cover for wildlife; also try to leave some short stems to mark your plants. At Dunham Massey there are problems with tree leaves blowing into the water, so the stems help to trap them.

If growing shrubs for winter stems, like *Cornus alba* 'Elegantis-sima', *C. stolonifera* 'Flaviramea' or *Salix alba* 'Britzensis' (syn. *S. alba* 'Chermesina') for example, then now is the time to cut these down to 1–2in/25–50mm in height for regrowth next month.

With the site clear, take stock of the weed problem. It cannot be over-stressed how important it is to start with a clean site. However, the problem of perennial weeds may be inherited. It is often the case that the weeds start into growth before your plants and so it may be a good moment to spray with a herbicide like glyphosate whilst you can, but remember to avoid spraying plants you wish to keep if they show any signs of green growth. The only other way is to fork the weeds out, including your plants if they are entangled.

Mid March

Waterside plantings do not tend to require the regular splitting and dividing encountered in conventional herbaceous borders; however there will be a need to reduce those which take an over-zealous liking to your allotted space. It may also be necessary, from time to time, to revitalise tired crowns by splitting them, or just a need to increase a favourite plant. Whatever the reason, now is the best time for most division – the plant has only to survive the shock for a short spell before warmer weather restarts growth. The chances of survival are greatest and re-establishment is quicker.

Mid to late March

With the border clear of weeds and untidy growth, and any split-ting now completed, we should see active signs of growth at various stages of advancement. This heralds the arrival of spring and raises the question of nourishment.

Nutrients should only be applied when growth commences, otherwise leaching may occur into adjoining water, increasing build-up of algae in subsequent months. For this reason I tend to avoid adding fertilisers unless historically the plants show deficiency. If used, fertilisers should be slow-releasing types, such as organic hoof and horn, or the new polymer-coated compound fertilisers.

Fork through the border, attending particularly to those areas most compacted, applying a 2in/50mm layer of mulch over the soil as you work your way off the border. Mulching is the greatest contributor to successful maintenance, particularly for waterside gardening. It provides the right rooting environment, suppresses germinating weeds and mosses, reduces soil moisture variations, cushions the soil from compaction during subsequent necessary activities (ie staking, dead-heading and further weeding), provides cover for slug predators (ground beetles etc) and last, but not least, vastly improves the overall appearance of the site. We use well-rotted cow manure, but there are many others just as good.

Plants that provide interest in March

Petasites fragrans (Winter Heliotrope) – flowers from January through to March, with lilac/pink scented flowers borne profusely on short stems, followed by large round long-stalked leaves. This is one for the wilder garden since it is a rampant grower. Similar, but less vigorous, is the later *Darmera peltata* (Umbrella Plant) with flowers in soft pink spikes up to 30in/76cm and round leaves held umbrella-like on top of 4ft/1.2m stems.

Caltha palustris, our indigenous Marsh Marigold, always succeeds in brightening March watersides with its yellow waxy flowers held above low hummocks of rich green foliage. There are also white and double forms. The early primulas include *Primula rosea*, a vivid rose red, followed closely by the Drumstick Primula, *P. denticulata*, with its short blue/lilac or white rounded heads.

The Skunk Cabbages are perhaps the most startling of the early spring flowers, the huge yellow arum-like spathes of *Lysichiton americanus* or the white of *L. camtschatcensis* stand erect before the huge cabbage-like leaves emerge in April. The true and aptly named Skunk Cabbage, *Symplocarpus foetidus*, is even earlier but needs careful placing due to the individual aroma of its purple-hooded flowers.

For striking foliage, grow *Iris pseudacorus* 'Variegata' (Variegated Flag Iris), and *I. laevigata* 'Variegata', at their best when newly emerged in early spring. The olive green and purple spears of the vigorous buttercup *Ranunculus lingua* 'Grandiflorus' and the bursting crowns of ornamental rhubarb, *Rheum palmatum*, also provide a burst of uninterrupted colour and interest in the following months.

TIP

Always moisten the compost of pot-grown plants before transplanting, teasing out the roots and discarding the top $\frac{3}{4}$in/2cm of compost to reduce the risk of 'importing' weed seeds.

APRIL
TO
JUNE

ROCK GARDEN PLANTING AND UPKEEP

Andrew Sawyer, Head Gardener

CRAGSIDE HOUSE · ROTHBURY · MORPETH · NORTHUMBERLAND

The romantic wild and woodland setting of this Victorian mansion was created by the vision of Lord Armstrong, the industrialist and inventor who built Cragside. There are over 1700 acres of woodland, a pinetum with outstanding specimens of North American conifers and a recently replanted rock garden which extends over 3 acres.

Observation and attention to detail in the rock garden are most important at this time of year, as plants come out of their winter rest into spring growth.

Pests and disease

Not only do the plants become active in spring; pests that feed on them are also making themselves known! Aphids can go almost undetected, especially in alpine plants with tight rosettes where the tightly-packed leaves make an ideal breeding place. As temperatures start to rise, slugs also become active. These creatures can wipe out an alpine treasure in one evening's dining. Be aware of these pests and take the necessary action to eradicate them as soon as possible.

At this time of year, rising temperatures and a damp atmosphere make ideal conditions for the spread of disease. Make sure plants are clear of any dead or damaged material and get rid of any leaves or debris not cleared up over the winter.

Reviving the plants

For plants which have died in the centre over winter, either mix a compost of equal parts loam, leaf-mould and sand and top-dress the remaining material; or lift the whole plant and replant pieces from the outer edge. Plants lifted by frost should be firmed back into contact with the soil and if necessary removed, a new hole dug and the individual replanted to ensure good contact with the soil.

Preparing the ground

April is a good month for planting, with the soil still moist from the winter rains and beginning to warm up, ensuring active and rapid root growth. But before planting up a new rock garden or replanting an established one, make sure all perennial weeds have been eradicated. It is essential to deal with pernicious weeds like Ground Elder, couch grass and horsetail *before* introducing valuable plant material. If need be, leave the area fallow for up to a year to ensure these weeds are destroyed; this will save time and a lot of heartache in future years.

Planting

Having established a clean planting site, ensure that the alpines will have well-drained yet moisture-retentive soil by adding leaf-mould and grit. The soil should be fertile, but strong manures and fertilisers should be avoided; the organic slow-release fertilisers are by far the best. Planting should be done carefully, making a hole large enough to accommodate the roots comfortably. Gently firm the soil around the roots to ensure good contact with the surrounding soil. Immediately after planting give a thorough watering and repeat when necessary while the young plants are becoming established.

Mulching and weeding

Many alpines, especially silver and hairy-leaved subjects, do not like to have their leaves in direct contact with the soil. A mulch of stone chippings or grit, in harmony with the rock used, keeps the vulnerable collar (the area between root and top growth) of the plant dry and keeps the leaves off the soil surface. The rock garden should be kept clear of weeds which can quickly out grow the small and delicate subjects planted there. This is best achieved by careful hand-weeding, which also gives the opportunity to view this marvellous group of plants at close quarters.

TIP
When pruning – think before you cut and cut with a purpose!

SOFT FRUIT

Stephen Biggins, Gardener-in-Charge

CALKE ABBEY · TICKNELL · DERBYSHIRE

The extensive walled gardens to the south-east of Calke Abbey constructed in 1773 were divided into the flower garden, the physic garden and the kitchen garden. In the restored physic garden, a wide range of fruit and vegetables is grown, including many old varieties. The pleasure grounds that extend beyond are carpeted with bulbs in spring.

During the month of April, soft fruit plants will demand your attention and require a certain amount of care to ensure bountiful crops in the coming season.

Raspberry canes

New raspberry canes can still be planted in April, then pruned to 6in/15cm above the ground. Raspberries are shallow-rooted so will extract most nutrients from a heavy mulch of farmyard manure at planting time. The need for both support and protection from birds and squirrels must be considered when planting and space allowed for these structures.

The flavour of the old variety 'Lloyd George' is unequalled, but the old prime minister is susceptible to cane blight. The Malling varieties might prove less troublesome.

Strawberry runners

Strawberry runners can be planted in spring, up to mid-April, but must then be de-blossomed in the first year. Early cropping strawberries under cloches could enjoy a little fresh air on a bright and sunny day. 'Royal Sovereign' is a delicious tasting old variety that you might like to try but, remember, old favourites can often be less resistant to pests and diseases than more recent introductions. Always buy certified virus-free stock.

Maybe the place to dabble with these older, more unusual fruit varieties is the smaller garden, where the commercial pressure of maximum crop yields is less of a consideration. Why grow in your own back garden a variety of strawberry or raspberry that you can buy cheaply in a supermarket? Experiment a little – take a risk!

Check for any winter die back or bird damage to gooseberries, red- and white currants and prune accordingly.

Weed control

If possible, avoid the use of any herbicide on the soft fruit bed. A weed-free environment can be achieved without resorting to chemicals if you are prepared to hand-weed and hoe. If fruit is planted into a plot cleared of weeds, it should not be too difficult to tease out the odd invasive perennial weed with a trowel or small spade. Annual weed seedlings can be controlled easily by using a hoe on a dry day.

Protection from birds and squirrels

Birds and squirrels are very likely to attack soft fruit, in particular strawberries, raspberries and redcurrants, whose juicy red fruits are irresistible targets. The better the protection given to the crop, then the better the chances are that the gardener will harvest more than the birds and squirrels. Now is the time to consider which method to employ, rather than wait until summer to run around the garden like a human scarecrow.

Ideally the whole plot should be caged over at a working height throughout the year, but this is a tall order for many gardeners. Manufactured frameworks and netting are widely available and work well, but might prove too expensive for a gardener with only the odd bush or two. The gardener-handyman could quite easily construct a framework using materials to hand which would be just as effective as long as the netting is in good condition and well secured.

Localised netting is effective for a small number of bushes; simply draping netting directly over the bush or canes greatly reduces interference from pests. Thin strips of tin foil can be hung from a string tied over the fruit bushes. Birds will be put off when the strips rattle in the breeze, squirrels unfortunately will not. Alternatives are bird scaring tape that emits a humming sound in the breeze, and Scaraweb, a spider's web-type fabric that can be gently teased onto the bush and is especially effective against bullfinches.

Control of pests and diseases

It is unrealistic for gardeners to assume that a soft fruit crop will remain pest- and disease-free throughout the season. Correct pruning and good nutrition will produce healthy plants which are less susceptible to pests and diseases. Nevertheless, one must inspect the crop almost daily in spring to be on the look out for the first tell-tale signs of trouble that will only get worse as the temperature rises. Identification of pests and diseases is only the first problem; the real trouble arises when deciding what methods to employ to combat these problems.

Chemical insecticides and fungicides of all kinds are available in great quantity on most garden centre shelves. 'Alternative', or 'organic' or 'environmentally friendly' products are also becoming more widely available and will perhaps appeal to those gardeners who feel uneasy about using chemicals on their fruit plots. It is not for me to suggest to others the course of action they should take; all that one can do is to identify the problems and use whatever spray one chooses, according to one's own philosophy and feelings.

Blackcurrants are the only bush fruit attacked by big bud mite which causes a swelling and a rounding of the bud. The mites emerge from the bud from mid-March to mid-April and invade adjacent buds. Light infections can be cut out but badly infected plants should be removed completely and destroyed. Control can be effected by spraying with an approved pesticide.

Be ever vigilant for the first symptoms of mildew and leaf spot on gooseberries which will increase as the temperature rises in May and June. The first sign of aphids is not uncommon on the growing tips of young shoots. Perhaps a systemic insecticide is the remedy. Choose an approved brand.

Aphids can also attack strawberries in April, so a suitable insecticide should be employed. Spray against leaf spot and leaf blotch, and check for any mould, especially on those plants under cloches.

TIPS

1. Avoid the use of all sprays whilst the fruit is in flower; all insects will be at risk and some are useful. Pollinating bees will be in particular jeopardy.

2. Avoid the use of pesticide sprays as the harvest approaches. Read the manufacturer's literature to establish exactly how long the delay between spraying and harvesting should be.

PLANTS IN CONTAINERS

Jimmy Hancock, Head Gardener

POWIS CASTLE · WELSHPOOL · POWYS

The 25-acre garden at Powis Castle has a terraced area, a nineteenth-century woodland area and a twentieth-century Edwardian formal area, all planted on different levels and allowing for a great variety of effects. Plants in containers are an outstanding feature of the Italianate terraces, thought to have been designed by William Winde between 1688 and 1722.

Plants in containers have been used in the garden at Powis from very early on. Care has to be taken in placing the containers so that they complement the surroundings. The choice of container, the type of material used and its size and shape are therefore important.

Choosing a container

Early plantings would have used lead urns, but earthenware materials are more practical and satisfactory these days. I prefer to go for good-sized containers; they do require big, bold displays to balance them but, provided the area can take it, this is all the better.

What to plant

Shape, size and foliage should take precedence over floral display. I aim for simplicity, and sometimes a single cultivar will be sufficient, but it is more usual to use around three different types of plant to get good height and spread. The other important point is to get plants of a good size early enough in the season so that by early April there is young vigorous growth capable of taking full advantage of the increasing daylight.

Propagation

Most of my propagating material comes as cuttings; these are taken any time after early August to get the desired size of plant by the following April. Once they are well-rooted, they are trayed up and kept in cool conditions to maintain firm and steady growth. The mid-winter period (December to January) is the most tricky time because light conditions are so poor. Temperatures should remain low – we keep our minimum temperatures between 37° and 28°F/3° and -2°C – and the trayed-up plants should be kept on the dry side. The plants can then be potted on, and as light conditions begin to improve there will be perceptible growth from mid-February onwards. At this stage we use 1-1½-litre pots; these should be filled with roots by early April when they will be placed in their containers. With the exception of unrooted cuttings, we use a John Innes formula compost, using our own turf to provide the loam.

Combinations of plants

Each container takes 7–10 plants, using combinations of *Bidens ferulifolia*, *Canna iridiflora*, *Datura cornigera* 'Knightii', *Diascia rigescens*, *D.* 'Salmon Supreme', *Felicia amelloides* forms, *Fuchsia fulgens*, plus other forms and cultivars, *Helichrysum petiolare*, *Iochroma lanceolata*, *Plumbago auriculata*, *Pelargonium* 'Mrs Kingsbury', *P.* 'The Boar' and *Tropaeolum majus*, 'Hermine Gnashof '.

Any staking is carried out in April, by which time all the real work has been done and we can sit back and enjoy the results.

TIP

It is always useful to keep a photographic record of your container plantings. Otherwise it is all too easy to forget after a few years how you achieved an effect that you liked and want to repeat.

GARDENING ON A GRAND SCALE

Frank Thomson, Head Gardener

STOWE LANDSCAPE GARDENS · BUCKINGHAM · BUCKINGHAMSHIRE

This idealised classical landscape was created in the eighteenth century for the Temple family, who employed many of the leading architects, sculptors and landscape gardeners to pioneer the revolution towards the more naturalistic landscape of grassy vistas and informal planting. Capability Brown was head gardener at Stowe from 1741.

To all of us who own or manage large gardens, April is probably the most challenging month of the year. Before us stretch months of work keeping Mother Nature at bay, or at least in some sort of order. If winter has been unkind, the threat of making even more mud has kept us from all those jobs that we promised to do before the next season. April gives us a chance because the ground is quick to heal itself at this time of year.

Planning ahead

I always try to think ahead. Those areas that always look untidy because an old stump or hollow prevents you mowing? This is the time to remove it or fill it. The trees that were planted in the autumn need mulch, weedkiller or tree mats. Completing all these little jobs now could save work during the coming months.

Mowing

There is no need to hurry the first mowing of the season and it is lovely to see the fresh growth and the wild flowers. In many areas a cut can be put off until late May, or early June. If the cuttings can be removed, this late cut will give you the benefit of the wild flowers, will reduce the fertility and thereby increase the flowers for the next season.

Repair work

April is a good time to repair paths and drives. During the winter, salt and frost play havoc with tarmac, so filling in pot holes now saves expense later on. Gravel paths which may have suffered over the winter cannot be repaired until the ground dries out.

Water gardens and lakes should not need much attention. However, pulling out fallen branches and removing some of the overgrown waterlilies and reeds at this time is easier and does not disturb the wildlife as much as it would in the summer.

Any bare patches of ground soon turn green at this time of year. If done now, grass repair should only involve scratching the surface with a rake and a light sowing of seed.

Providing colour

Where possible, sow hardy and half-hardy annuals directly into the ground where you want them to flower, to provide colour throughout the summer. You will avoid the expense of buying bedding plants and save time by not having to plant them out.

Some years one is tempted by the mild weather to put out the plants that have been nurtured over the winter. Don't risk it; late frosts are almost bound to come along and in their weakened state tender plants hardly ever survive.

Reaping the benefit

In all this rush of work in the spring do not miss the chance to admire what is happening around you in the garden. Nature's beauty at this time of year is a sight not to be missed.

TIP
The secret of gardening, and especially gardening on a large scale, is to work with nature not fight against it; try to tame rather than dominate.

COASTAL GARDENING

David Mason, Gardener-in-Charge

COLETON FISHACRE GARDEN · COLETON · KINGSWEAR
DARTMOUTH · DEVON

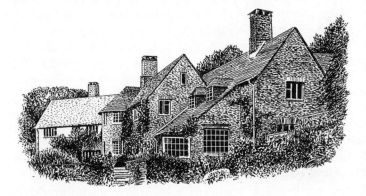

*Lady D'Oyly Carte created the garden at Coleton Fishacre between
1926 and 1940 to complement the Lutyens-style house. Situated near the
mouth of the River Dart, it benefits from its mild, sheltered and relatively frost-free-position and since the National Trust acquired the
garden in 1982, the plant collection has been considerably expanded.*

The combined effects of the Gulf Stream and the protection
afforded by shelter belts against the prevailing winds mean that it
is possible to grow outside a wide range of unusual and exotic
plants which are more commonly found in a glasshouse or
conservatory.

Shelter belts

The key to successful coastal gardening, whether on the eastern or
western seaboard, is protection from the prevailing winds. The
climate of the coastal region will obviously determine the types
and varieties of plants grown, but without an adequate shelter belt
many plants will succumb to the detrimental effects of salt and
dessication, or will suffer damage from the velocity of the wind.

No matter what the scale of your garden, the maintenance of a healthy permanent shelter belt is imperative. This may involve thinning and replanting established woodland, or replanting and pruning to restore an old hedge, or replacing and repairing artificial barriers, such as fences and screens, which provide vital shelter to new plants as they get established. Evergreens are best for shelter belts, since they give all year protection, although some deciduous trees and shrubs, such as blackthorn and hawthorn with their close-knit twiggy growth, can be interspersed successfully in hedges.

Planting the shelter belt

April is a good month to plant evergreens for the shelter belt, while deciduous plants should have been planted during the winter in their dormant period. When planting always use compost and a general fertiliser to help the plant get established. If the spring is a dry one, remember to water regularly until the plants have produced enough roots to be self-sufficient in stressed conditions. Suitable evergreens include conifers, evergreen oaks, *Escallonia*, *Olearia* and *Tamarix*. It may also be necessary to build individual shelters for certain prized specimens. For these, you need nothing more elaborate than bamboo canes, stakes or branches covered with netting or some similar 'fabric' which 'breathes' and lets light through.

Danger of late frost

With a mild climate and extended growing season, certain plants will produce new growth early in the year and last year's growth may have failed to ripen from lack of summer sun. These plants are particularly susceptible to the unexpected late frosts that can occur in April and catch everyone unawares. Young shoots will be burnt back and flower buds lost, especially on camellias, magnolias, acacias and cestrums. Be prepared; one sunny day does not mean that winter has passed. If frost is forecast and protection is only required overnight, then a light blanket or old curtain is acceptable.

Supporting plants

My practice is to stake where I feel it is necessary; but the crucial thing is to plant small trees or plants so their root systems develop strongly as they grow. However, it is important in a garden susceptible to wind damage that plants are suitably supported. This applies not just to newly-planted specimens which have not yet developed a root structure, but to vulnerable old favourites too. Use a stake appropriate to the plant's size together with suitable tree-ties. With the onset of the new season check all staked plants, adjust ties to allow for new growth and for any loosening during the winter months.

Suitable plants

The closeness of the sea at Coleton Fishacre means that humidity is high, an atmosphere which is not conducive to rose-growing. The roses originally grown in the Rill Garden have been replaced with half-hardy perennials, including osteospermums, salvias, argyranthemums, cannas and several beautiful hybrid hedychiums or ginger plants. The warm, well-drained south-facing hillsides and terraces are ideal for such plants as yuccas, *Beschorneria yuccoides* from Mexico and echiums from the Canary Islands. There are Californian lilacs, New Zealand brooms and cistus from the Mediterranean.

Climbers and wall shrubs

The house walls and walled garden provide ideal conditions for climbers such as the sweet-scented Chilean jasmine and the white potato vine – *Solanum jasminoides* 'Album'. Among the wall shrubs are *Fremontodendron californicum*, which has large bright-yellow flowers, and *Nicotiana glauca*, an outstanding plant which also does well in a conservatory. Trained against the wall, its bluey-green foliage and small yellow trumpet flowers are delightful. It grows very vigorously and requires autumn pruning to take off any whippy growths which might catch winter winds.

The abundance of natural water in the valley below the house provides warm humid air for plants such as tree ferns from New Zealand and bamboos from China. The spring-flowering embothriums with burnt red-orange flowers and *Gevuina avellana* with its shiny pinnate leaves and white flowers flourish here, with their roots in moist shade and heads in dappled sunlight.

TIP

Although your garden may not be suitable for the unusual trees and tender and exotic southern-hemisphere shrubs that we grow at Coleton Fishacre, many would make excellent conservatory plants.

FAVOURITE OLD RHODODENDRONS

Fred Hunt, Head Gardener

STOURHEAD · STOURTON · WILTSHIRE

Stourhead is a magnificent eighteenth-century landscape garden created by Henry Hoare around a long artificial lake to provide, with its temples and follies, an English version of Arcadia. The rhododendrons planted in the nineteenth century give a stunning early summer display.

The rhododendrons at Stourhead are mainly hybrids and there are over 100 named varieties, so it is only possible to pick out a few favourites, some of which are ideal for medium-sized and large gardens.

Early rhododendrons

The season starts with 'Christmas Cheer', a compact bush with pink flowers fading to white with dark green foliage. Another early one is 'Nobleanum Coccineum', deep red in colour, which flowers from January until March, depending on the weather.

From March the crimson *Rhododendron barbatum* is in bloom. It is easily recognised by the small beards at the leaf bases and the attractive brown bark.

Spring and summer

April to May is the peak flowering time for rhododendrons. I consider *R.* 'Loderi King George' one of the best; it grows up to 20ft/6m in height, has huge trumpets of scented pink flowers fading to white, and attractive new growth after flowering. 'Loder's White' is another very good rhododendron, making a large bush with candle-like pink buds opening to white flowers.

R. 'Britannia' is a medium-sized bush, with trusses of glowing scarlet flowers; very compact, it is suitable for the medium-sized garden. *R. auriculatum*, *R.* 'Polar Bear' and *R. diaprepes* flower throughout July and are well worth having if you have the room. They are large and tree-like, growing to 20ft/6m in height with creamy-white scented trumpets of flowers. If possible, plant in a lower position as they are very attractive to look down on. The yakushimanum hybrids, or small-growing azaleas, are suitable shrubs for the small garden, providing the soil is correct (*see p.60*).

Layering

The problem with the older varieties of rhododendron is that they are becoming more difficult to obtain. We layer wherever possible. After flowering select a branch growing near the ground, scrape the bark underneath and secure it to the ground with a wooden peg. Cover with soil and after about two years it will have rooted. Sever the branch, dig up the new plant carefully and plant elsewhere.

Care and maintenance

To establish rhododendrons the balance of the soil must be correct – an acid soil with a pH of 5.5 is ideal. They also require some shade as they are shallow-rooted and dry out very quickly in a hot season. Rhododendrons also suffer from scorch to the flowers and leaves. Mulch small plants with rotted leaf-mould until they are big enough to shade their own root system. Little pruning is required, especially on well-established bushes. Simply remove dead wood and straggly growth, take off dead flowers very carefully and occasionally feed with rhododendron fertiliser.

With the right treatment, especially when newly planted, rhododendrons will give many years of flowering, and require very little attention.

TIP
Wherever possible, remove dead heads from rhododendrons after flowering.

GARDEN POOL MAINTENANCE

Andrew Humphris, Gardener-in-Charge

THE COURTS · HOLT · NR TROWBRIDGE · WILTSHIRE

This 7-acre garden created by Lady Cecilie Goff in the 1920s is full of surprises: one half is more formally divided by yew hedges, shrub borders and raised terraces; the other includes an arboretum planted with spring bulbs, an orchard and hazel coppice. Other features include a lily pond, pleached limes and a conservatory.

Waterlilies can soon overcrowd a pool, and leaves and debris build up in the bottom if not removed annually. Spring is the ideal time to split or replace over-vigorous waterlilies and to clean out any debris that may have collected in your pool.

First things first

Before emptying the pond take precautions to avoid harming the wildlife. If there are frogs or toads in the pond there will also be spawn and young at this time of year, in which case do not clear the pond until September. If there are fish and the pond is small, use a net to catch them. Otherwise, wait until the water has almost drained away and then just pick them out by hand. In both cases put the fish in a large tub of water until the pond has been cleared and refilled. If there are newts, pick these, too, from the almost empty pond and keep them in a large bucket of water.

Drain or pump the water from the pool and remove the waterlilies, oxygenators and any marginal plants. If you have noticed a mound of small leaves in the centre of a waterlily, and the flowers seem to be becoming smaller and fewer, then it

61

definitely needs splitting. Ideally, all the leaves should be flat on the surface of the water.

Splitting plants

The waterlily rootstock consists of a main rhizome with a number of sideshoots. Each sideshoot will produce a single healthy plant and should be removed using a sharp knife. The shoots may then be planted into pots of heavy loam and placed in containers with enough water to cover the pots by 2–3in/5–7.5cm. Split the marginal plants in the conventional way, by using two garden forks back to back, and retain them in water in the same fashion as the waterlilies. Keep all of these to put back into the pool.

Cleaning

Next, remove the silt and debris in the bottom of the pool. If you allow the pool to dry out for a few days beforehand, this task will be considerably easier.

Using tubs

For most pools it is best to grow waterlilies and marginal plants in tubs which can be placed in the pool wherever you want them. The tubs help to control the spread of the plants, make removal and division of the waterlilies simpler, and allow for easier movement if you decide a plant should be in a different position. For larger and more naturalised pools, waterlilies may be planted directly into a layer of loam on the bottom, or into loam which is contained behind small retaining walls to create beds.

Refilling

Once the waterlilies and other plants have been put back into the pool, immediately refill it with water. Rainwater is ideal, but otherwise tap water will do. The water will almost certainly turn green due to algal growth which thrives when there is little competition for sunlight and the abundance of nutrients provided by the fresh water. This is a normal occurrence in newly-cleaned ponds.

When the waterlilies have established themselves, their leaves will provide shade on the water's surface. Waterlilies, oxygenators and marginal plants will all be using nutrients from the water, thus depriving the algae of nutrients. It may take up to a season but the water will eventually clear.

Maintenance

Netting should be placed over the surface of the pool to stop leaves and debris collecting in it in the autumn. This will remove the need to drain and clean your pool again for many years.

TIP

In future years, remove and split half the plants in the pool annually. In this way the established plants should cover enough of the pool to keep the algae in check and also provide plenty of flowers each year.

WEED CONTROL WITHOUT CHEMICALS

Barry Champion, Head Gardener

TRELISSICK · FEOCK · NR TRURO · CORNWALL

An outstanding feature of this sheltered garden near the estuary of the River Fal is its collection of rhododendrons, azaleas, hydrangeas, camellias and flowering cherries. The only fig garden owned by the Trust is here and the mild Cornish air encourages the growth of exotic palms.

It is certainly true that a chemical-free weed control programme requires more physical effort in the early stages, but I am convinced that there is no advantage in the use of chemicals in order to save labour. There are four important prongs of attack in a chemical-free regime; mulching, regular hoeing, weeding assiduously so that weed seed never sets and starting with clean ground.

Mulching
Mulches are used to exclude light and prevent weeds germinating.

- ☐ Black polythene is a very satisfactory inorganic medium for the suppression of annual seedlings and is the most effective mulch to eradicate perennial weeds, but is not attractive if exposed.
- ☐ Biodegradable polythene works in the same way as black polythene but in theory will decay and can be rotavated or dug back into the soil after cropping. I would not use this in an ornamental garden unless an organic mulch was put on top for aesthetic reasons. Confine it to the vegetable garden.

- Stone/slate chippings or shingle are acceptable in some flower gardens but are not as effective as organic mulches.
- Newspaper can be used as an organic mulch, mainly in kitchen gardens. Any mulch remaining can be dug into the soil after cropping. Not that successful a method.
- Home-made compost is good although, depending upon the ingredients, it could be reserved for use in the soil rather than on top. It might contain a certain amount of weed seed unless very well made. (*See also* COMPOST MAKING, *p.135*.)
- Grass mowings need to be quite deep in order to be effective; they tend to rot down anaerobically, becoming smelly and slimy. Use in compost rather than as a mulch.
- Farmyard manure is an excellent mulch but can contain large quantities of weed seeds.
- Mushroom compost contains lime and should not be used on ericaceous plants. Apart from that, it is visually and aesthetically very good as well as being free of weed seeds. Its rapid breakdown uses up nitrogen which must be applied in the form of fertilisers.
- Wood chips and shredded prunings are an excellent mulch. It is best to compost them for 2–3 years first, then apply. Their direct use around objects is acceptable but the mulch will have to be supplemented with a general fertiliser high in nitrogen to replace nitrogen lost during decomposition.
- Bark is the most aesthetically pleasing of all mulches. Completely free of weed seeds, different grades can be used for different requirements. It has one major disadvantage – cost.
- Leaf-mould is the most important mulch in a woodland garden, although primarily best for potting composts. Ericaceous plants thrive in it. It is, after all, nature's mulch.
- Peat/coir is a good mulch and soil conditioner, but the use of peat is no longer environmentally acceptable.

Hoeing

Regular hoeing is of prime importance even if there are no obvious signs of weed seedlings. The effect is the same as providing a soil mulch. A dutch hoe is best in these circumstances although it is a tool that requires skill to use; start at one end and work backwards with a to and fro movement so that the end result is in neat rows and you do not walk over what has been hoed. With a draw hoe, a forward chopping movement is used so that the hoed area is walked over and you run the risk of trampling weeds back into the soil.

Preventing weed seeds setting

It is very important not to allow weeds to set seed. Everyone will recall the old adage: one year's seed, seven years' weed.

Starting with clean ground

Your ground should be cleared completely by digging, removing weeds as you go. The more pernicious weeds, couch grass and ground elder, are more easily controlled with herbicides. It will take several years to eradicate them manually but it can be done. Annual weeds can be turned into the soil or in subsequent years composted. The use of cleansing crops, such as potatoes, on ground you have just cleared is highly recommended.

Most gardeners take a responsible attitude towards the environment and I hope this brief introduction to organic gardening will encourage you towards this rewarding approach.

TIP
For the successful establishment of newly-planted rhododendrons, remove all flower buds before they develop. All the energy will go into producing side growths and root development rather than seed. (*See also* FAVOURITE OLD RHODODENDRONS, *p.58*.)

HARDY FERNS

Malcolm Hutcheson, Head Gardener

SIZERGH CASTLE · NR KENDAL · CUMBRIA

Built in 1926 from Westmorland stone, the rock garden at Sizergh Castle is now an impressive size. Streams and rock pools allow moisture-loving plants to flourish and there is an exceptional collection of hardy ferns.

It is often well into May before most hardy ferns awaken from their period of winter dormancy and unfurl their fronds or crosiers of pale green, brown and bronze.

Where ferns grow

The natural habitat of the hardy fern is very varied, ranging from the tiny Adder's Tongue (*Ophioglossum vulgatum*) of short turf and the small Maidenhair Spleenwort (*Asplenium trichomanes*) found in crevices in walls and rock faces, to the tall fronds of the Royal Fern (*Osmunda regalis*) found in bogs and sand slacks of remote wet, acid areas. Most are deciduous, but a few, like the shield ferns (*Polystichum*) and wall ferns (*Polypodium*), are evergreen.

With this wide variation of growth, plus their relatively simple requirements for cultivation, hardy ferns are once again popular as garden plants. The Victorians appreciated their value as a good green foil in their gardens, with many forms and cultivars being discovered or propagated by that generation of fern enthusiasts. Alas, a great number of fine forms are now extinct, and only occasionally does a good form reappear in long-established or neglected gardens.

Conditions

Hardy ferns tolerate most conditions found in the average garden and are very useful in providing a greensward in difficult areas, like under trees in dry shade. Lady ferns (*Athyrium*) and male ferns (*Dryopteris*) along with the evergreen Soft Shield Fern (*Polystichum setiferum*) do well in these sites. Most fern species will grow in difficult open sites, like the foot of a north-facing wall,

or in wet conditions by ponds or streams. Some of the smaller species, like the spleenworts (*Asplenium*) and in the more sheltered garden maidenhairs (*Adiantum*), do well in rock gardens, favouring sites in rock crevices or in rubble screes.

FIG. I

You can find fern species to suit all types of soil conditions with *Dryopteris* (*fig. 1*), *Cystopteris* and *Polystichum* growing in shallow limestone soils, whereas *Athyrium, Blechnum* and *Thelypteris* will thrive in more acid soils. Even wet peaty conditions will suit *Blechnum* and *Osmunda*.

Propagation

Propagation can be accomplished either by growing on young plants from spores that requires a little time and care, or by simple division. Division of a clump of fern crowns (rootstock) is the same as with general herbaceous plants – use two forks back to back, breaking out the individual crowns of the plant. A 5-year-old plant will often produce 3–4 crowns. The job can be tackled at any time of the year, although the best time for division is early spring before the fronds unfurl. For the best effects, planting is done using groups of 5–7 crowns. The soil is prepared by adding leaf-mould or some humus-rich compost with coarse river sand to improve soil structure.

Some of the shield ferns (*Polystichum*), particularly large mature specimens, regenerate themselves vegetatively by producing tiny plantlets at the joints of the pinnae on the fronds. These fronds are pegged down with a small stone and covered over with a light dusting of sand/peat mixture, which should encourage the parent frond to decompose and the small plantlets to root into the compost.

Propagation by spores is rewarding if a little care is taken. In the late summer most species will release spores from the spore clusters on the undersides of the fertile fronds. Collect the spores as the clusters turn rusty in colour by removing part of the frond and placing it in a paper bag. After a few days the spores will dry out and will be like dust at the bottom of the bag. They are best sown straight away, but are viable for several years. (see fig.1)

Prepare a 4–5in/10–12cm pot with crocks and good drainage and fill up with potting compost to within 1in/25mm of the rim. Sift a fine cover of compost on top to ½in/13mm of the rim and place a piece of kitchen paper over the surface. Make the soil and the pot sterile by pouring boiling water from a kettle carefully on to the paper and allowing the water to seep slowly through the compost. When the pot has cooled down, remove the paper and sow your spores. Cover the pot immediately with either a clear polythene bag or cling film. This prevents the surface area being contaminated by other spores. Place the pots in a cold frame or under the glasshouse staging, shading them from direct sunlight.

Boiling water to sterilise compost and pot

Kitchen tissue

Glass or clingfilm

Spores

Seed compost

Good drainage

After a month, a green mould or prothallus will appear on the surface. Do not remove the cover at this stage as this is a crucial time in the young ferns' development. Ten weeks on the first tiny fronds will be developed enough for the polythene cover to be removed. The young plants can be pricked out into trays, keeping them damp and cool. Pot on when required.

TIP

Ferns really are an enormously versatile group of plants. Do bear this in mind if you have a particularly difficult place in your garden. A fern could well be the answer!

SUMMER BEDDING

Chris Tolley, Head Gardener

WADDESDON MANOR · NR AYLESBURY · BUCKINGHAMSHIRE

Baron Ferdinand de Rothschild created the garden surrounding the French Renaissance-style château at Waddesdon in the 1880s. There are 165 acres of parkland and formal gardens and the spring and summer bedding schemes on the fountain terrace provide spectacular displays.

Summer bedding has been used in many historic gardens both large and small from the mid-nineteenth century until the present day. Generally, the larger Victorian gardens had the facilities and staff to handle hundreds or even thousands of plants in many contrasting colours. As gardening staff numbers shrank, the fashion for summer bedding waned. Fashions have changed again and with increasing interest in all things Victorian, summer bedding is once again popular. Private gardens are now much smaller, but there is ample scope for quite eye-catching displays using many of the newer generations of plants that are available from local garden centres.

Tender plants

Summer bedding plants are raised either from seed or cuttings through the winter months to be in peak condition for planting in early June, depending on the prevailing conditions. Tender bedding plants cannot withstand frost and cold winds, so are removed from the borders generally by mid-October. Seed companies are always trying to improve already well-established varieties. Regular trials are conducted by horticultural bodies to monitor and compare quality and weather resistance.

Home-grown bedding

Like all gardening achievements, more enjoyment is gained when the plants are 'home-grown'. Prepare your summer display by studying the seed catalogues for spring-raised plants. A hot greenhouse is not a necessity and a home-made cold frame in a sheltered corner will do as well. Even a sunny windowsill will help seeds to germinate quickly. Try covering the pots with cling film to help raise the temperature of the potting medium.

Many of the large bedding plants, such as pelargoniums and dwarf dahlias, can be lifted and stored dry in a dark shed. Better still, take cuttings in late September to nurture through the worst of the winter. Always take more cuttings than you think you will need to offset losses, any surplus can be given to friends.

Preparation

Preparation of the planting site is always important. Dig to a good depth, working in well-rotted manure or compost made from your own garden waste material; this helps improve the soil condition and will provide food for the plants as well as help retain moisture in a dry season. If a winter planting of polyanthus, pansies and bulbs is planned, dig thoroughly when pulling out the old plants. Working a little bonemeal into the fine surface soil is a long-established practice to provide a natural food source.

When to plant out

As spring slips into summer, don't be tempted to plant out too early as a late frost or cold wind will ruin your carefully grown plants. Garden centres tend to offer soft bedding plants too early and limp lobelias and mangled marigolds will result. If you have purchased all your plants this can be expensive, so do wait until the chances of a late frost have gone.

Grouping by colour and height

Summer bedding using lobelia, impatiens, marigolds, fuchsias, ageratum, dahlias and geraniums can look good as a feature in their own bed or at the front of herbaceous borders where they give density to planting in areas which can often look thin. Group plants together without overcrowding; the display is much better and weeds will be crowded out. Instead of a mixture of colours, try groups of blue, pink, golden-yellow and red and try planting in bands with taller plants to the rear of your display. To heighten the effect introduce architectural plants with 'sword-like' foliage. Cordylines and hardy yuccas, to use as single 'dot plants', are available with green, bronze-tinged or variegated foliage.

Planting in pots

Containers such as tubs, urns and window boxes provide opportunities for colourful planting. Try some of the new double petunias which have ruffled edges to the flowers. They are available in a wide range of soft colours.

The majority of these plants are for high summer, but new varieties of pansy are available to flower all through the winter in a range of blues, whites, mauves, reds and yellows. Winter sunshine on these plants helps to brighten the garden at a very dull time of the year.

TIP
After planting out, dress finely crushed bark around the plants as a mulch to retain moisture and control weed seedlings. The rich dark brown is a good background to your colourful summer display.

WILDFLOWER MEADOWS

Mike Snowden, Head Gardener

ROWALLANE GARDEN · SAINTFIELD · BALLYNAHINCH · CO. DOWN

Very little landscaping was carried out in these 52 acres of garden by Hugh Armytage Moore who developed it over 50 years from 1903. Determined to find a place for a plant, as opposed to a plant for a place, the informal planting follows the lie of the land. Established on the fields of a hill farm, many rocky features are incorporated in the garden.

In days gone by, June meadows were colourful with flowers growing amongst the grasses, which after reaping provided winter feed for farm stock. Many of these rich areas have long gone but your garden may have a place where a smaller version of a meadow could be created. As well as providing added interest in your conventional garden, a wildflower meadow attracts butterflies, birds and small animals that rely on flowers and grasses as food sources. An orchard, the difficult bank by the drive or roadside, the poor patch of soil that will not grow anything, could provide the site.

Preparing the ground

Ground of low fertility is the key to success. If the site is too rich, reduce the fertility by removing the top 2–3in/5–7.5cm of soil to the vegetable plot where its value may be put to better use. Lightly cultivate the exposed surface to form a seed bed. Allow time for deep-rooted weeds to grow and remove or treat them with herbicide. September is the ideal time to have the seed bed

73

ready to sow. The soil is warm and there is less chance of it drying out under hot sun as autumn days approach.

What to sow?

There are a number of seed companies that produce mixes of flower and grass seed (the grasses are as important as the flowers). Choose a mix that will suit your soil; is it sandy and light or clay and heavy, acid or alkaline? Keep the conditions of the site in mind; is it shady, damp, dry or exposed? There are mixtures to match most situations; remember that in nature there are few places where nothing grows.

How to plant

Sow thinly and shallowly, as most of this type of seed is naturally shed on the surface and may need light to germinate. Then be patient; you are creating something that in the past evolved over many years of man's management of the land. Following these management patterns is the way to succeed. Through the autumn the plants will establish themselves and by spring will be well away. By late May the plot will be ready for its first cut. Do not cut it too short at this point; leave 3in/7.5cm to prevent the grasses lying over and smothering the flowering plants before they have formed strong root bases. Cut at this height two or three times during this first year even if a few flower spikes appear. If possible take these cuttings off and add to the compost heap. The following year all should be well-established.

Cutting

By April primrose and cowslip will be flowering; during May the cuckoo flower should be seen in the damp spots and many flower spikes will be forming to open in June. This is the traditional time for hay-making. If your meadow is growing well, watch to see when the spring flowers have set seed, usually around the last week of June. This is the time to cut, but again not too short so as to avoid damaging the plant base. Let the cuttings lie for a day or two; the seeds will fall out and the herbage cure for use as hay or put it on the compost heap. This is also the time to cut down the foliage of daffodils naturalised in grass.

How often to mow

If you wish, the area may now be mown regularly, but not too short, for the rest of the growing season. This is the equivalent of the meadow being grazed by farm stock. The alternative is to let it grow again, allowing late summer flowering. The second cut is carried out around the end of August or early September. If the fertility of the soil is low you can miss the June cutting, taking one crop in September.

The pleasure of wildflower meadows

Now for one of the supreme joys of a wildflower meadow. Rake your hay into haycocks, put down the rake and sit with your back against one of them, then lean back, half-close your eyes as you look up at the sky and take in the scent. As you doze off I swear you will hear the song of a skylark, the swish of the scythe and the distant chatter of a horse-drawn reaper.

TIPS

1. To establish wildflowers in existing grass, raise flowers from seed in pots. Spray glyphosate onto small areas of grass 12in/30cm square or remove turf. Plant 5–7 flowers in each patch.

2. If you cut fuchsias at the end of winter, save the twigs to use as support amongst tall annuals or in the herbaceous border.

USING SEMI–TENDER PLANTS

Andrew Mudge, Head Gardener

KILLERTON · BROADCLYST · EXETER · DEVON

Through Killerton's connections with John Veitch, the famous nurseryman who was originally the land agent to the estate, the garden has for three centuries been the recipient of new species from all over the world, including many rhododendrons from the Himalayas. The herbaceous borders were laid out in the early 1900s by William Robinson.

The range of semi–tender plants, sometimes called 'patio plants', available to the gardener is vast and new varieties seem to appear each year. They range widely in colour, shape and habit. Many semi–tender plants are perennial, such as penstemons, diascias and some of the salvias, but they are more vigorous and more flori-ferous if new plants are propagated each year.

Hardiness

Hardiness is largely dependent on which part of the country you live in and also, most importantly, the site. If the site is chosen carefully it is surprising how hardy some plants are. Ideally most should be grown on free-draining soil with a south-facing aspect. They do not tolerate wet soil or very windy situations.

Groupings

Semi–tender plants are best displayed in bold groups in one border. They are very good at replacing the traditional summer bedding, as a stop gap in the herbaceous border and they can also be used with very good effect in containers and hanging baskets.

Placing semi-tender plants in the garden can be difficult and needs a bit of thought as some of the colours can look harsh and out of place. They fit in much better when planted *en masse* in a border, where it is much easier to grade the colour. For example, the bright reds of *Salvia elegans*, *Penstemon* 'Castle Forbes' and the bright orange of *Calceolaria* 'Kentish Hero' can gradually give way to the softer colours of *Penstemon* 'Hidcote Pink' and the pale lilac of *P.* 'Alice Hindley' and on to the yellows of *Osteospermum* 'Buttermilk' and *Argyranthemum* 'Jamaica Primrose' through to the blue felicias and salvias, finishing with the whites and grey of *Argyranthemum frutescens* and *A. foeniculaceum*. Many plants have grey foliage and this can often be used as a link from one plant to another. Heights can also be used to good effect, ranging from 5ft/1.5m salvias down to the low-growing diascias and gazanias, enabling you to create an undulating mass of colour.

The flowering period is a long one. Semi-tender plants are probably at their best during June and July, but they will flower from planting out in May through to the harder frosts in November and December.

Attention

Once planted out in the garden, these plants need little attention; no staking is required and watering is only necessary in the early days until they are established. No feeding is required, apart from a bit of organic material worked into the soil. If planted into a soil that is too rich, there will be excessive foliage growth at the expense of flowers. After the main flush of flowering, dead-heading is beneficial and will help keep the plants flowering over the period. Pest and disease problems are few.

Propagation

Propagation is relatively simple; soft cuttings taken in late summer and placed in a propagator with a cover are perhaps the simplest way and they will root very quickly. However, they do need to be overwintered in a frost-free glasshouse or frame.

Semi-tender plants are a very worthy addition to any garden and will give enjoyment to anyone who grows them.

TIPS

1. If you take the trouble to dead-head your semi-tender plants as it becomes necessary, your reward will be a better and longer display.

2. A pot with a plastic bag over the top makes an effective propagator.

JULY
TO
SEPTEMBER

HERBS
ON THE MOVE

Paul Gray, Head Gardener

GUNBY HALL · GUNBY · NR SPILSBY · LINCOLNSHIRE

Situated in one of the most remote corners of England, these old redbrick walled gardens are planted with traditional vegetables, fruit and flowers. The herb garden flourishes profusely and there is a massive Cedar of Lebanon planted in 1812.

Herbs are very special plants; they are beautiful as well as useful both in the kitchen and as an extension of the medicine cabinet. There are few sights in the garden as pleasing as butterflies and bees enjoying the good life of the herb garden on a hot summer's day.

Tolerance

Whether your herb garden is half an acre or just a few plants in a trough, herbs always look their best when young and fresh. Fortunately, most herbs are native to this country and are not as prone to as many garden 'nasties' as some of their more exotic flowery cousins. Being strong and robust, they tend to tolerate poor soil, bad drainage and drought. So perhaps a herb garden is the ideal garden to have? Regrettably, many people have started herb gardens and found this is not so.

Failure and success

The main reason for herbs failing is, ironically, their own success. Two or three years from planting, the whole plot can become a tangled mess, or become overrun with one particularly success-ful plant; spearmint is a good example. Another reason for failure is that the shrubby types of herb, like sage, rosemary and rue, tend to get sparse and woody after five years or so, looking thin and straggly near the base and generally past their best. Some, like cotton lavender, will respond to hard pruning at the right time of year. At Gunby, we have found over the years that the secret of success is to keep replanting and moving herbs. Initially, this may sound daunting, involving lots of hard work and expense, but it need not be the case. Herbs fall into three main categories: annuals and biennials, herbaceous and shrubby.

Annuals and biennials

The annuals and biennials like basil and parsley are simple enough to grow from seed and discard when finished. Try not to grow the same annual on the same piece of ground each year.

Herbaceous herbs

The herbaceous herbs, eg mint, marjoram and chives, are perennial but go dormant over winter. The problem with most of the herbaceous varieties is their spread rate. Deal with their excessive growth by splitting the clumps regularly, even yearly if the plant is growing well. The time to do this is in the autumn or spring after the plant has filled all its available space, but don't wait until it has completely overwhelmed its neighbours. Splitting is done by forking out the whole clump and selecting an outside piece of root and eyes, usually as much as will fill a 5in/13cm pot. This will be retained for replanting and the rest can be discarded once most of the soil has been removed. While looking to see what has got out of control, it is also a good idea to note where there are plants of similar height and appearance. When it comes to replanting, ideal places can be swapped around so that the newly split plant is not in the same soil as its parent. This is good policy but not essential unless there have been plant health problems.

Shrubby herbs

Shrubby herbs, like rosemary and sage, can be deciduous or evergreen. For these herbs we usually strike cuttings 5in/13cm long in a 50/50 peat/sand mixture, with 7 to a 5in/13cm pot. These are overwintered in a cold frame and potted into a 3½in/9cm pot in March and a 6in/15cm pot in July. This will give you a good strong 2ft/0.6m high plant by the following spring. The ideal is to take cuttings from a shrubby herb at its peak, not after it has become shabby. By doing this you ensure you have good young plants to replace older ones before they have 'gone to seed'. Again, if possible, try to swap positions when replanting.

TIP

For the best flavour, pick herbs for drying before they flower. Tie them into small bundles and hang them head downwards in a cool, dry place.

THE UPKEEP OF
MIXED BORDERS

Penelope Hobhouse, formerly Tenant Gardener

TINTINHULL HOUSE GARDEN · TINTINHULL · NR YEOVIL · SOMERSET

This tiny, delightful walled garden is divided into separate areas by clipped hedges and the different 'rooms' thus formed include an azalea garden, a fountain garden and a kitchen garden. Two opposite beds in the formal pool garden contain planting schemes that are strikingly contrasting in colour.

Borders of 'mixed' planting – a combination of tender and hardy plants and shrubs – definitely require high maintenance, with lots of essential annual tasks, all of which need implementing at fairly exact moments in the gardening timetable. By July, however, all the work that is necessary should have been done earlier in the season and there is relatively little to do except enjoy the results. The tasks in July are minimal: remove dead flower-heads and fading leaves, and prune back flowering branches of shrubs such as philadelphus and deutzias.

Care and attention

Each type of plant needs attention at some time during the year. Shrubs need pruning – sometimes twice annually, once after flowering to remove flowering sprays but also in winter when attention is paid to the general shape and the promotion of new growth. All herbaceous plants, which grow from winter dormancy at ground level to a peak performance in just a few months, need rich feeding, plenty of water (especially in the early growing season), and staking and tying in individual groups as required in early summer. Some also need dividing in the latter part of the season or as the ground warms up in spring. I prefer doing it in spring; experience at Tintinhull has proved that this works best. I do not find it necessary to split plants up as often as many books recommend.

What to plant

Annuals grown from seed and tender shrubby plants grown from cuttings and treated as annuals are invaluable for bulking up colour schemes; they are put out after the last predicted frost. Spring bulbs, such as tulips, scillas and camassias, which make a setting for the emerging herbaceous foliage, are planted in the autumn and can be worked in between perennials which flower later in the summer, as well as under the branches of deciduous shrubs. Summer-flowering bulbs, such as acidantheras (*Gladiolus callianthus*) and summer hyacinths (*Galtonia candicans*), which take the scheme into the autumn are planted in April and need full exposure.

Coping with drought

The most important single task, which will reduce any need to water during times of drought, is to mulch very thoroughly in spring when the water table is high. At Tintinhull we use home-made compost, mushroom compost or leaf-mould if available. I never use chipped bark. We mulch as we plant in March and April but also add mulch round the last annuals put out in May. If you do this thoroughly, having originally dug and prepared the soil with plenty of rich humus-making organic compost, borders will survive long periods of drought.

Changing colour and shape

However, the success or failure of the scheme depends on something more than general maintenance. To keep your border beautiful you need to juggle plants around every year. The best blueprint is only a guide to original planting. Plants grow at different rates so that the relative proportions of shapes and colours are constantly altering.

TIP

It is in July that you can assess the scheme; I like to take quite detailed photographs for viewing when making alterations, and plan for next season's enjoyment.

CUTTING HEDGES

Peter Dennis, Assistant Head Gardener

HIDCOTE MANOR GARDEN · NR CHIPPING CAMDEN · GLOUCESTERSHIRE

Created from 1907 onwards by Lawrence Johnston, this 10-acre hilltop garden is an intriguing blend of ordered formality and artless confusion. Hedges of box, yew, holly and hornbeam contain and connect the compartments of the garden, each of which has a distinctive character of its own.

The traditional deciduous plants used for hedging, hornbeam and beech, are usually trimmed once a year, beginning in July after the main flush of growth has been made, leaving only a short time before growth ceases. The traditional evergreen hedging species of yew, box and holly are also trimmed once a year, but slightly later, during late August or early September. This is to guard against a late flush of growth not ripening before the onset of winter and damaging frosts. Other hedge plants which grow more vigorously, such as privet, hawthorn, lonicera, and leylandii, will need cutting more often as their growth demands.

Equipment

Hand shears are suitable for small areas as long as they are strongly made and of the type with a 'waved-edge' blade profile, not the straight-edged cutting shear. If a large amount of hedge has to be trimmed on a regular basis, or hand shears are found to be tiring, some form·of powered trimmer is the answer. Machines driven by electric motors are popular and are probably best suited to most people's requirements. They come in varying cutter-bar

87

lengths and it is worth bearing in mind that short bars are far less fatiguing than long ones, with about 18in/45cm being most suitable. For rough hedges and those far from a power source, petrol-driven cutters are the answer, but they are noisy, smelly, dirty and heavy to use for any length of time.

Shape and size

Hedges can be of any shape or size, but the shape that is often recommended has the profile of a flat-topped A. This is supposed to allow better light levels at the base, which should prevent the basal growth becoming thin and weak. Another reason for using a narrow-topped profile is apical dominance, a characteristic of the growth of many plants. Shoots at the top of the plant suppress by hormones the growth of shoots down below. So the more growth your hedge has at the top, the less it will have lower down. Hedges with broad tops are likely to be thin and ragged at the base for this reason.

The main pitfall to avoid is the top of the hedge becoming wider than the base, because then the top growth becomes loose, prone to snow damage and the hedge mass splits. Aim for a height that gives the required privacy and windbreak effect and can be managed easily from a small pair of steps. The width should also be kept to a minimum that allows dense growth and is easy to reach across while trimming, without stretching and straining.

Once a hedge has reached its required height and width, it should be rigorously kept to these bounds. To do this, when trimming, follow the stubs of the previous year's cut. Whenever possible it is important not to allow any longer shoots to remain – if an inch or two of growth is left on each year it will become a foot within a few seasons, and drastic action will have to be taken to bring the hedge back under control.

Achieving formal lines

If it is necessary to impose a straight line on a formal hedge, lines and plumbs can be used. Far simpler is to trim by eye, but it does require great care. Very gradually cut away the rough growth, frequently checking from the end of the hedge that a line can be viewed through as a level surface. Go over the hedge again, removing any growth that stands out in the line of sight. This process is repeated horizontally. Although this may seem an uncertain and imprecise method to produce a very formal effect, it is the surest technique. If the plumb-line alternative is used, often the fall of the ground or hedge appear to run at an angle. If you work to what appears to be true to the eye, the effect will be acceptable visually even if it is not correct mathematically.

TIP

A well-fed hedge is a healthy hedge, so apply a reasonably thick dressing of well-rotted farmyard manure to an established hedge. Not only will this feed the hedge but it will suppress any weeds growing beneath it.

WALL FRUIT

Ted Bullock, Head Gardener

FELBRIGG HALL · NORWICH · NORFOLK

The delightful walled garden of this seventeenth-century house has espaliered fruit trees, vines and figs trained on the walls and beds with dahlias, roses and herbaceous plantings. In autumn the National Collection of Colchicums in the shrub borders makes a spectacular display.

The soil at the base of walls and fences, especially those facing south, can be exceptionally dry at this time of year and fruit trees trained against them must have adequate water. Newly-planted trees and established pears are particularly susceptible to dry conditions.

Need for light and air

Do not allow tall herbaceous plants or shrubs to crowd trained wall trees; provide an adequate space, at least 3.2ft/1m, in front of the trees to allow in light and air, and for the application of mulches in the autumn.

Dealing with trusses and suckers

The June drop of apples should have thinned out the crop considerably but if the trusses still appear too crowded, snip away any surplus fruit with scissors. Sucker shoots arising from the bases of trees can be easily pulled off now; do not use secateurs because the shoots can regrow with a vengeance.

Pruning

Start summer pruning this month to maintain the shape of trained trees and control their vigour and fruitfulness. Removing a proportion of foliage has the effect of checking a tree's growth, at the same time letting in sunlight and air which improve the colour and quality of the developing fruit. Whatever kind of fruit tree you are tending, remove all dead, diseased and damaged shoots first. Check all tree ties to ensure they are not too tight; replace broken ones and add more if necessary.

Apples and pears

Cordon and espalier apples and pears have their side shoots pinched or cut back to within 5 leaves of their base; fruit buds can develop on the shortened shoots, these being further reduced next winter to 2 buds from their base. Do not prune leading shoots now, especially if a tree has yet to fill its allotted space; they are pruned back by about one-third in winter in order to stimulate the growth of new extension shoots.

Stone fruits

July is the safest time to tend stone fruits such as gages, cherries, peaches and apricots. Avoid winter pruning because of the risk of silver-leaf disease. Pruning stone fruits can be daunting at first and it is helpful to have an understanding of the fruiting habits of the various trees. Young side shoots are best controlled by pinching and stopping.

Sweet cherries carry their fruit on spurs on older wood and pruning usually consists of pinching back the tips of the side shoots to about 5 or 6 leaves.

Acid cherries carry fruit on long shoots produced in the previous summer; these are removed after fruiting so the aim when pruning is to provide a supply of replacement shoots to tie in their place for next season.

Gages and plums are borne on spurs produced on old wood and also on short shoots of last summer's growth; their side shoots are pinched back to about 5 leaves and any arising directly from the front of the branches are best rubbed off. Peaches and nectarines fruit chiefly on shoots produced in the previous summer; these are cut out after fruiting and new shoots, selected earlier in the year, are tied in the gaps.

Apricots are treated in a similar fashion, but since they can also bear fruit from spurs on older wood, a proportion of sideshoots are pinched back to 6 leaves to encourage spurs to form.

Trouble-shooting

Do not summer prune any trained fruit tree which looks poorly. Try to diagnose the problem, which may be due to lack of water or nutrients, or perhaps a pest or disease, then set about restoring the tree to good health.

TIP

When ordering an apple tree for wall training, ensure the variety is a spur and not a tip-bearer. Three good spur-bearing varieties are Cox's Orange Pippin and James Grieve (dessert) and Bountiful (cooker).

IN THE KITCHEN GARDEN

Christine Brain, Head Gardener

BARRINGTON COURT GARDEN · NR ILMINSTER · SOMERSET

The 1920s design for the gardens at Barrington Court was based on an earlier plan by Gertrude Jekyll, with three 'rooms' providing separate colour themes. The splendid walled kitchen garden contains trained wall fruit and a cornucopia of vegetables.

August in the kitchen garden is very much a time of harvest, when the fruit of the year's labour is literally being gathered both from the trees as well as the ground.

Fruit trees

The protected environment of a walled garden provides the ideal situation for trained fruit trees and one of the most important late summer jobs will be pruning, both on trees that have already fruited as well as those yet to mature. Peaches and nectarines will be ripening in August. Older fruited wood can be removed once the fruit is gathered, young growth tied in to replace this and ensure good wall coverage. Light pruning of plums and gages can also be tackled.

Restricted growth of cordon and espalier forms of apples and pears is achieved by summer pruning, reducing the current year's growth to about 6in/15cm. This is further reduced in winter to 2–3 buds. (*See also* WALL FRUIT, *p.90.*)

Soft fruit

Soft fruit will by now have been harvested and pruning will be necessary on blackcurrants to remove the fruited wood, leaving the new young growth to carry the fruit next year.

Raspberries that have already fruited will need attention. The prickly task of cutting out the old fruited canes and tying in the new growth is best done as soon as possible, before the canes become brittle and less pliable. Autumn-fruiting raspberries will be starting to ripen by the end of the month and make a valuable extension to the soft fruit season. They bear fruit on the current year's wood so are easily pruned in midwinter by cutting to ground level.

Strawberry runners should be planted in August if they are to be established successfully before fruiting next year. If plants are free of virus and disease, it is a straightforward operation to root your own runners. If at all doubtful about a plant's health, buy in certified stock to ensure good plants. The soil should be well manured before planting the runners, ensuring that the crown is at soil level to avoid rotting. (*See also* SOFT FRUIT, *p.46.*)

Pegging strawberry runners for rooting.

Vegetables

Harvesting will be the main task in the vegetable garden with so many seasonal and salad crops maturing in August. Lettuces, tomatoes, cucumbers, radishes and beetroots, as well as runner and French beans, peas, new potatoes, carrots and spinach, are all reaching their peak as the month progresses.

Seed of salad crops can still be sown in early August to give lettuces, radishes and beetroots in early autumn. In the south-west of England, Japanese onions can be sown on well-prepared ground to give mature bulbs ready to harvest early the following summer when they are valuable for filling a gap.

TIP

Protect peaches and nectarines against bird damage by draping netting over bushes. A peck on the fruit from a bird will create an ideal site for wasps and bees to land and destroy it.

COMPANION PLANTING

John Teevan, Head Gardener

FENTON HOUSE · WINDMILL HILL · HAMPSTEAD · LONDON NW3

An oasis in north London, this small, walled and terraced garden is a delight. There are seasonal herbaceous borders edged with box; bulbs, scented herbs and perennials, such as rosemary, lavender and dianthus, mix happily together; the orchard has a selection of mature trees and there is a kitchen garden with an abundance of vegetables.

I once overheard a visitor to a National Trust property asking the gardener what he thought of garlic as a companion plant. The gardener replied that the visitor wouldn't have many companions if she chewed that stuff!

Before fertilisers and pesticides

Although the gardener obviously misunderstood the visitor's question, it is an indication that companion planting is not widely practised nowadays. However, in the days before fast fertilisers and pesticides were invented, farmers and gardeners noticed that certain plants grown in proximity to food crops improved their health and vigour. Recently, further investigation has begun to support these beliefs which were previously thought to be based on folk-lore.

Some examples of companion planting

The curse of potato growers, the eelworm, can be deterred by a secretion in the roots of the French marigold, so potato beds can benefit from a few of these. In the same way, the exudate from grass roots growing too close to an apple tree can adversely affect the development of the tree. The flavour, vigour and disease resistance of strawberries can be noticeably improved if a blue-flowered borage is grown nearby.

Garlic and roses

The maligned garlic appears to act as a deterrent against aphids when planted near roses. I tried this on a rose which covered a high wall and was difficult to spray properly. Aphid infestation was indeed minimal. The only slight problem was that the garlic tended to die off, deprived of sunlight by the surrounding herbaceous plants. Perhaps this method should be avoided in a rose garden as the pungent odour of masses of garlic would impair the delicate fragrance of the roses themselves.

Attracting hoverflies and lacewings

Planting flowers to attract these insects is an effective way of dealing with aphids. The aphid armies are decimated by the adults and, in particular, the larvae of hoverflies and lacewings. These insects, with their short feeding tubes, are attracted by the more open-structured blooms such as nasturtiums, poppies, marigolds and feverfew. Cabbage white butterflies beam in on the smell of maturing brassicas and become confused by the aromatic oils of herbs such as rosemary, thyme and hyssop planted among them. Similarly, onions alongside beans, carrots and cabbages emit a more powerful odour and deter aphids and rootfly.

Cottage-garden effect

Another example of companion planting is to mix ornamental flowers with vegetables and so camouflage the host plants. Pinches of hardy annual seeds, such as clarkia, nigella and clary, scattered about at sowing time will perhaps offend the ordered eyes of the rigid row devotees but will produce the more romantic cottage-garden effect. Foxgloves are recommended by herbalists as the friends of all other plants and clumps of these stately blooms on the margins of a vegetable garden can play the part of benevolent sentinels.

Vegetable gardens

A plant that has been cut down can also benefit other plants. The roots of cut down legumes enrich the soil with nitrates which greatly benefit leafy plants such as cabbages and lettuces. The decomposed weeds in the compost heap disperse their accumulated minerals to grateful recipients.

A vegetable garden with its overall backdrop of subtle greenery can be enormously enhanced with the bright and colourful embroidery of companion planting in both the practical and aesthetic sense.

And finally...

I will leave the last word on companion planting to a friend of mine who claimed that hawthorn planted in his fruit garden dramatically increased the yield of his fruit trees and bushes. He'd placed the thorny barrier strategically between his property and the adjoining school!

TIP

Grow mint in a bottomless container at the end of carrot rows. Baffle the carrot rootfly, when thinning the crop, by rubbing handfuls of the fragrant mint leaves together and sprinkling them along the rows.

ORGANIC PEST CONTROL

Julie Schofield, Technical Assistant

THE NATIONAL TRUST · CIRENCESTER

The staff at the National Trust's offices at Cirencester comprise specialists who give regular advice to more than 160 gardens and landscape parks of varying size, character and style in the care of the Trust.

Gardeners have for centuries waged war on the pests and diseases which destroy crops and ornamental plants. Methods of control have varied over the years, reflecting our changing knowledge of chemicals and of the pests themselves. In recent years chemicals have been used in greater quantities than ever. Many are residual, which has led to worrying accumulations in food chains. This has prompted many people to look again at organic methods of controlling pests which were used successfully in earlier centuries.

In the glasshouse

Biological control uses natural predators to destroy certain pests. This practice was first recorded in AD300 by Chinese fruit growers who introduced ants into their citrus groves to eliminate caterpillars and beetles. Biological control is most effective when used in the manageable environment of the glasshouse. Today a dozen commonly used predators are available by mail order and increasingly at garden centres. They control most common pests, for example, whitefly, which is parasitised by the tiny wasp, *Encarsia formosa*, and red spider mites which are destroyed by the predatory mite *Phytoseiulus persimilis*. Other garden insects, such as ladybirds and lacewing larvae, eat greenfly and can be used as biological controls by bringing them into the glasshouse.

Aphids

Greenfly are perhaps the most common glasshouse pest; one Victorian solution to the problem was the invention of the 'aphis brush' or 'greenfly destroyer'. It took advantage of the aphid's natural tendency to drop off a plant when disturbed, which makes the idea worth copying today. It is easy to dislodge mild infestations of aphids from delicate leaves and shoots with an old toothbrush.

Another, more modern, method of catching aphids, whitefly and other flying pests is to hang sticky yellow cards just above the plants in the greenhouse. The insects are attracted to the bright colour and then become stuck to the card.

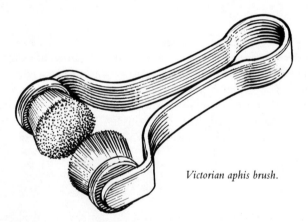

Victorian aphis brush.

Red spider mite

The red spider mite thrives in dry conditions, so numbers can be kept down by regular humidifying of the glasshouse in hot weather. In 1803 William Forsyth advised that on hot afternoons the glasshouse should be flooded until the water was several inches deep on the floor. The glasshouse was then closed down for the night allowing the water to evaporate and form a fine film of moisture over the leaves, so killing the mites.

In general, good hygiene in the glasshouse is the best way to avoid insect problems. Dead leaves and shoots should be removed and flower pots scrubbed before re-use to kill off pests and disease.

Outdoor controls

Outdoor organic controls are more tricky to implement because everything is on a much larger scale; however, the general rule about hygiene should be applied throughout the garden. Old leaves often harbour caterpillar eggs and dead wood will act as a host for many different disease-producing agents. Slugs and snails hide in crevices and in clusters under stones. Get into the habit of turning stones over and destroying the pests beneath. Where pests cannot be eliminated from the garden, they can be deterred from eating choice plants. For example, putting ashes around suscepti-ble plants is first mentioned in a fourteenth-century Arabic manuscript. Sharp grit or old holly leaves work equally well, making it difficult for the slug to reach the plant.

Animals in the garden

Biological control can be used to a certain extent by encourag-ing predatory animals into the garden. Bird-boxes will help to persuade insect-eating birds to take up residence, and they can be fed during winter months when insects are less easy to find. Hedgehogs can also be encouraged by building a nesting-box, and frogs and toads will often make their homes in a garden pond. All these creatures will help to reduce insect pests in the garden.

Earwigs

Earwigs can be a problem for chrysanthemum growers but control has not varied much over the years. In 1569 it was recommended that shoes stuffed with hay and left overnight would act as a hiding-place for earwigs which could then be killed. The Victorians used bundles of bamboo canes or old bean stalks, and today a flower pot stuffed with straw and turned upside down works just as well.

Dealing with moths

Codling moths often damage an apple crop. Pheromone traps hung in the trees to lure the males to their death can limit the damage. Strips of corrugated card tied around branches will attract pupating caterpillars and the card can be collected later and burned. Grease bands tied around a tree trunk are the modern equivalent of tying strips of sheepskin – wool side out – tight against the trunk of the tree. Both prevent wingless moths climbing the tree trunk to lay their eggs.

Resistant varieties

Crop rotation helps to break pest and disease cycles, as do resistant cultivars of plants. Some are now listed in seed catalogues. Much pioneering research is being done on the breeding of resistant varieties and an increasing number will become available.

TIP
A thorough autumn clean-up in the glasshouse is essential to get rid of overwintering pests.

GOING IT ALONE

Robert Ludman, Gardener-in-Charge

STANDEN · EAST GRINSTEAD · WEST SUSSEX

Designed by Philip Webb, a friend of William Morris, in the 1890s, Standen overlooks Weirwood Reservoir in the Medway valley with the garden built on several levels. The upper areas are planted with hydrangeas, azaleas and rhododendrons, there are some fine trees, good examples of effective ground cover and a delightful rose garden.

The title of this piece begs an explanation. The 12-acre garden at Standen is maintained by one person throughout the year plus a part-timer for half a day a week (and staff from Nymans who kindly cut the grass when the gardener is on holiday). This requires a totally pragmatic approach to the work schedule to ensure that the load is spread evenly throughout the year. By August the main aim is to enjoy a respite after the frantic months of May, June and early July. Anyone with a large garden to maintain will understand our approach.

Ground cover

By August the various ground cover schemes have knitted together to form a reasonably weed-free tapestry. These plant carpets also make an excellent mulch, thus preventing the sandy soil at Standen drying out. Particular favourites are the true geraniums, the various varieties and hybrids of *Geranium endressii* proving very useful for this purpose. *Hypericum calycinum* is good too, especially if cut back in early spring. Obviously hostas are excellent but Standen's most stunning and effective ground cover is the swathe of *Nepeta* 'Six Hills Giant' which surrounds the rose beds. Ferns are useful, though most need some shade themselves to grow well. Harts' Tongues can take drier conditions and are effective in making 'rivers' of shiny green, if the contours are right.

Lawns

The most dominant ground cover in many gardens is grass. By August large parts of the lawns lose their verdure because of the sandy soil and lack of shade. No watering is done; unless this can be continued frequently and heavily, it will do more harm than good. Lawns usually recover their green by mid-September. Thankfully it is then no longer necessary to mow lawns twice a week.

Trimming and pruning

All the hedges are cut at the end of June so they only require a light trim on a cool day at the end of August. Most of the hedge clippings are scrunched up by the rotary mower and left to disappear back into the soil. The rambling and climbing roses are usually pruned in August, but our large beds of Rugosas are maintenance-free until February when they are cut with a hedge-trimmer. Summer pruning of our old espalier apples is done early in August.

Weeds and disease

We try to keep ahead of weeds before they seed. Horsetail is a real problem and needs continual pulling if we are to be reasonably free of its unsightliness in August. We never need to spray roses against aphids in August as wasps do the job much more effectively. I think much rose mildew can be prevented by using Jeyes fluid (dilute 1 tablespoon of Jeyes fluid to 1 gallon of water or 4.56 litres) from a watering-can around each plant after leaf fall.

Working with nature

There is always plenty to do simply keeping the garden under control and the gardener is pleasantly busy in August. The joy of gardening at Standen is that we attempt to work with nature and not impose a rigid style or follow an inflexible timetable.

TIPS

1. Only water vegetables if they have flowers. Water is necessary on peas and beans if soil is dry when they are in flower.

2. Be careful with glyphosate. Though it is not harmful to the environment, it can kill any green plant it touches.

3. Take a tip from the broccoli growers in Cornwall and do not water in brassica seedlings immediately after planting out. They will put out roots to find the water.

DEALING WITH DAHLIAS

Nigel Davis, formerly Head Gardener

BIDDULPH GRANGE GARDEN · NR STOKE–ON–TRENT · STAFFORDSHIRE

now Head Gardener

SHEFFIELD PARK GARDEN · UCKFIELD · EAST SUSSEX

Biddulph Grange Garden is the most complete high-Victorian garden in Britain with many nineteenth-century features, including a spectacular dahlia walk. Sheffield Park is an eighteenth-century landscape garden of 100 acres, transformed early in this century with an exciting collection of rare and unusual trees and shrubs.

Dahlias were introduced into cultivation in the late eighteenth century from Central America. These single-flowered species – *Dahlia coccinea, D. merckii, D. variabilis* – rapidly grew in popularity so that by the mid-nineteenth century Victorian nursery catalogues listed thousands of varieties which had been developed from these. The favourites in those days were the 'Globe' and 'Ball' types, generally known then as the Double Show and Fancy Dahlias. The popularity of dahlias continues, although today it is the decorative and cactus-flowered varieties that are most widely grown.

Today, dahlias come in a wide range of sizes – from dwarf bedding varieties to giants taller than a man, with flowers ranging in diameter from tiny pompons the size of a two-pence coin, to huge exhibition blooms the size of a dinner plate. They are to be found in every colour except blue.

Dahlias in September

The dahlia year culminates with the glorious display in late August and September when the true value of the plants can be appreciated, and the fruits of all the past seven months' labours can be realised. There is no finer sight in the garden in September than a well-stocked dahlia border. September is also the time to take stock of newer varieties on the market. Go to major dahlia nurseries and see what they have on offer for the following year, or visit the dahlia shows held around the country and see what the 'showmen' produce from their dahlia plants.

Catching earwigs.

Dahlia tubers

The dahlia produces tuberous roots or tubers which enable it to perpetuate itself year after year. These tubers are normally lifted after the first frosts and overwintered in dry peat, sand or soil in a frost-free and damp-proof spot. The secret of storage is to make sure the tubers are free of soil, dry, and the fibrous roots carefully removed. As the flower stems are hollow, the tubers should initially be stored upside down to let any water drain out. Alternatively the stem can be cored out with a screwdriver to create a drainage hole.

The dahlia year begins when these tubers are started into growth in the spring by bringing them out into the light and warmth. The tubers can either be planted directly into their planting positions in late spring, or cuttings can be taken from the tubers, which are gently forced into early growth, and the rooted cuttings planted out in late May/early June after the danger of frosts has passed. The tops of the cuttings can be pinched out to encourage bushier plants.

Use in herbaceous borders

Dahlias can be grown in beds on their own, but can be used successfully to bridge the late summer colour gap in the mixed border. Wherever they are used, the taller varieties all need staking and tying. A 1in/2.5cm square stake should be placed behind the planting position before the dahlia is planted, to which the label can be attached. The stake needs to be shorter than the ultimate height of the plant. Two additional canes can be added to the front of the plant at a later date if required; these assist the tying up and supporting of the plant's foliage.

Care and maintenance

Once planted, dahlias need watering if conditions become dry, tying up and disbudding if you want top show-quality flowers. Dahlias are excellent for cut flowers, and in the right conditions a single plant can produce upwards of 60 blooms.

Fortunately, dahlias are not prone to major pest and disease problems if they are growing well and are not under stress. The three main pests associated with dahlias are slugs, earwigs and aphids, which can all be readily controlled. To trap earwigs, put a straw-filled plant pot upside down on top of a stake. Empty out each morning (*see illustration p.107*).

The diseases commonly seen are mildew, particularly on older varieties, and mosaic virus which causes stunted growth and yellowing of the leaves. The only cure for the latter is to lift and burn the whole plant. This should be done to prevent its possible transfer by aphids to other plants.

By the time September has arrived your dahlia plants should have reached their full height and be in full bloom. Enjoy them outside in their flowering positions, or cut some to decorate the inside of your home. The season is always too short, and an early frost will destroy the remaining blooms. It is then time to start the cycle of the dahlia year again.

1. The regular removal of faded blooms will prolong the flowering life of the dahlia plant.

2. In order to achieve larger (but fewer) flowers, it is necessary to remove the side buds, leaving only the terminal flower bud.

TOPIARY

Fred Corrin, formerly Head Gardener

PACKWOOD HOUSE · LAPWORTH · SOLIHULL · WARWICKSHIRE

now Head Gardener

BELTON HOUSE · GRANTHAM · LINCOLNSHIRE

The famous yew garden at Packwood is an arrangement of trees laid out in the seventeenth century and thought to represent the Sermon on the Mount. There is also a sunken garden with charming gazebos at each corner and fine herbaceous borders. Topiary also features in the garden at Belton House where the formal gardens were restored in the late nineteenth century.

History of topiary

The art of training, shaping, cutting and controlling trees and shrubs to create ornamental objects, hedges and archways, was introduced into Britain by the Romans, who used it in their formal courtyard gardens. During the Dark Ages, however, few gardens existed outside the monasteries, and even nobles lived within fortified settlements with little room for pleasure gardens.

Life had become more settled and peaceful by the late Middle Ages; the wealthy began to build fine mansions and surround them with formal pleasure gardens. These were made up of hedges and walled private gardens containing elaborate knot patterns using dwarf box and herbs and incorporating standard topiary, beasts, mazes and mounds. The formal style developed and peaked towards the end of the seventeenth century, during the reign of William and Mary.

Then came the landscape movement and many of these formal gardens with their unfashionable topiary were destroyed. However, formal gardens appeared again in the nineteenth century. By the end of the century topiary was popular not only in grand gardens but fine examples were grown in cottage gardens. Many of the specimens we see today were planted at the end of the last century or the beginning of this century.

Choosing plants for topiary

Many evergreen plants can be used for topiary but yew and box are ideal because they have longevity, dense thick foliage, can withstand training and pruning, and once established usually only require annual trimming. Quick specimens may be grown using privet, for example, which is not completely evergreen and will require several clippings throughout the growing season.

Creating the shape

Simple shapes like pyramids, balls and squares may be formed free hand, tying and trimming to produce the shape desired. Complex topiary may well require a basic framework through which the plant is grown and by trimming and tying into the framework, the final shape is achieved. Remember to give ample food to increase and encourage plant growth and replace the nourishment lost by clipping.

Clipping and tying

Established topiary requires regular clipping and possibly some degree of tying in to maintain the shape. Tie in any branches that have become displaced before commencing clipping. This is best done using tarred string on the small branches and rope on anything heavy. Do this in such a way that it is hidden by the

Topiary at Hidcote Manor Garden, Gloucestershire.

foliage and is not cutting into the plant. Check at this time that any previous tying material has not become too tight, restricting new growth and damaging the plant.

On very intricate topiary hand shears and secateurs must be used. On large and less intricate specimens electric shears may be used. These are light-weight and more comfortable to handle for long periods.

When cutting topiary, time must be taken to stand back and view the work frequently and from a number of angles to ensure that the correct balance and effect is achieved.

Safety

Wear comfortable protective clothing to prevent scratches and other injuries. Access to the trees or bushes may well require ladders and platforms (at Packwood we sometimes have to use hoists). Ensure safe and firm anchorage; ladders may need ropes attached to a number of fixed anchorage points. Do not be tempted to take chances! Only when the operator feels safe can he or she do the job with the necessary care and attention to detail.

Electric shears obviously represent a considerable hazard if great care is not taken to keep the cable away from the cutting blades. It is sensible, indeed a must, to use an electric-circuit breaker to prevent danger to life!

General management

All plants require weeding, watering and feeding. Feed during the growing season with a balanced fertiliser. Mulching is a good idea as this keeps down the weeds and reduces water loss if the weather is dry.

Watering during dry spells is necessary. If yew or box are planted in heavy clay soil the lawn must be adequately drained or the plants will be in danger of root damage and disease.

Winter care

Snowfall on topiary can cause considerable damage with the weight bending branches, sending them out of shape and sometimes causing them to break. Try therefore, as soon as possible, to knock off snow gently with a pole. Should damage occur, repair quickly by tying in and, if necessary, removing the broken branches to allow regeneration of new growth.

Treating neglect

Topiary which has been neglected will often require drastic pruning and re-tying into shape. Remove old dead wood. Remember healthy yew plants can be cut back to the trunk if necessary and will readily regenerate.

TIP

It cannot be repeated too often: you must check the position of the power cables, and where they are in relation to the cutters, just as often as you check the lines of the topiary you are cutting.

PLANNING AND PLANTING FOR SPRING BEDDING

Sam Youd, Head Gardener

TATTON PARK · KNUTSFORD · CHESHIRE

This 60-acre garden has been planted by four generations of the Egerton family, beginning in 1814 when the orangery was designed. Apart from the spring bedding display, the rhododendrons in May are spectacular and other unusual features are a fernery with huge tree ferns, a beech maze and a delightful Japanese garden.

There are so many flowers surrounding us in September that it is easy to overlook the need to plan and plant for a good spring display next year. If you have not raised your own plants for this purpose during May and June of the current year, then you will probably be buying in plants from garden centres.

Plant choice
When I choose plants I try to follow this checklist to make sure I buy the best:

- choose a plant with a compact, sturdy habit
- look for healthy plants which have good foliage colour, remembering that some spring plants are naturally paler in leaf colour, eg daisy (*Bellis*)
- if plants are potted, make sure they are not root bound
- try to buy plants which have been grown in open ground but watch that the roots have not dried in transit.

Likewise, when choosing bulbs they should be:

- good and plump with firmly intact skin
- free of fungi and physical damage
- dry, but not dried out
- slightly flexible when squeezed and not sound hollow.

Keep in mind that biggest is often best – the largest bulbs will have more flower power and will be less prone to virus and disease. Many of the cheaper varieties are the best choice, again for the same reasons; they are more vigorous and less prone to disease.

Preparing the ground

Good ground preparation is essential. Dig the area over, incorporating plenty of organic material. As well as improving the soil structure, this promotes rapid root development which is essential to plants in early winter.

If you are intending to grow wallflowers, then the ground and plants will benefit before planting from a dressing of lime at 2oz per sq yd/57g per sq m. The best time for planting will depend, of course, on how soon the summer bedding finishes.

If the summer has been dry, it is best to avoid planting until after a spell of rain. In areas where winter tends to be early, the earlier the spring planting is completed the better, so that plants settle in before the worst of the winter weather.

Plants

Most spring bedding plants can tolerate extremes in soil conditions but obviously some do better if planted in the correct place, eg daisy (*Bellis*) which is generally used for edging. Forget-me-nots (*Myosotis*) do best in moist soil and some shade; indeed, if they dry at the root they will suffer from mildew and spoil your display.

There are many very good new varieties of winter pansy. These need good soil and a sunny position. Polyanthus need a well-drained soil and I find it best to plant them with their crowns just a bit higher in the soil than they were previously planted. They then pull themselves into the soil by means of their anchor roots. This planting method avoids rotting in the crown of the plants. When planting, make sure that plants are firmed well in and always firm plants back in after heavy frosts. Take precautions against slugs.

Subjects

The most commonly used plants in the spring bedding display are daisies, forget-me-nots, pansies, polyanthus and wallflowers. In addition to these, it is worth using tulips, daffodils, hyacinths and muscari (grape hyacinths). Various combinations can be put together and tastes differ but some of my favourites are outlined below.

Combinations

I like mixed polyanthus which give a tapestry look to the bed, fronted by a soft blue edge of forget-me-nots with an extreme edge of the pinky-white daisies.

With wallflowers it is best to have beds of single colours which will all flower at the same time and make a more dramatic impact. I also think that beds of single-colour wallflowers, such as 'Blood Red', go well if they are interplanted with single tulips like 'Keizerskroon' which is bright scarlet and deeply-edged with yellow. The important point to remember about interplanting tulips is that you should go for a variety that flowers just above the wallflower plants (about 14in/35.5cm).

I would be cautious about using the tall Darwin Hybrids unless the site is very sheltered. It can be heart-breaking to find all the heads broken off by spring winds after waiting so long for them to flower.

Tulips can be used for special effects, eg Kaufmanniana and Greigii types, which not only have interesting flowers but have mottled foliage. The other advantage is that they only grow to between 5–7in/13–18cm high which makes them very useful for containers, particularly on patios.

Another group of some interest are the Viridiflora tulips which flower in May – the flower colour, as the name suggests, being predominantly green which is rather unusual. They grow about 16in/40.5cm high so need a little shelter.

TIP

To discourage 'fire' disease in tulips (scorching of the leaf edges), lift and store the bulbs every year after the leaves have died down. Do not plant tulips in the same bed year after year.

EXOTIC PLANTING

Tony Murdoch, Head Gardener

OVERBECKS · SHARPITOR · SALCOMBE · DEVON

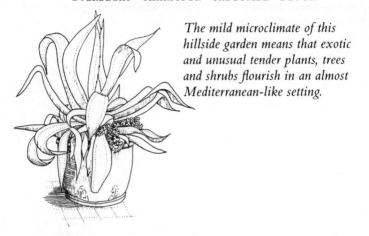

The mild microclimate of this hillside garden means that exotic and unusual tender plants, trees and shrubs flourish in an almost Mediterranean-like setting.

Gardening in South Devon, where bananas have been grown outdoors for more than 50 years, can be adventurous and some colourful borders can be created.

Grouping for effect

Planning is essential. Use groups of tall architectural-leaved plants strategically placed to provide a structure which can be filled with plants of good shape, form and colour.

To create an effective background use groups of large-leaved plants of tropical appearance such as bananas, cannas, phormiums and cordylines. Hedychiums have beautifully scented flowers as well as good foliage.

Subjects

At Overbecks we have different varieties of phormiums – New Zealand flax. Their brightly-coloured leaves enable us to achieve stunning colour combinations. Here we have *Phormium* 'Firebird' with red leaves against the silver-leaved *Astelia* 'Silver Spear' and the black foliage of *Ophiopogon planiscapus* 'Nigrescens'. *Phormium* 'Maori Maiden', with its pink leaves, contrasts well with the really exotic *Aeonium* 'Zwartkop' with its deep purple, flat dinner-plate heads.

Yuccas, especially the golden variegated varieties, combine with *Cordyline australis* 'Purpurea' and the variegated variety 'Albertii'. Another similar spiky plant, which has most exotic striking red and green flowers and yucca-like foliage, is *Beschorneria yuccoides*.

Other plants which could be included in an exotic border are *Melianthus major*, mainly grown for its ornamental foliage, and *Euphorbia mellifera* which also has good foliage. The perfume from its honey-scented flowers casts a spell over a wide area.

Echium pininana is another recommendation. It flowers during the second year and has blue flowers on a stem which can reach 15ft/5m in height. The plant dies after flowering but not before 'popping' its seeds to provide plants for the future. Datura, with its spectacular trumpet-like flowers, is yet another popular exotic plant.

Perennials

If shape, form and colour of foliage are considered important, but the individuals you chose lack the attraction of brightly-coloured flowers, then groups of tender perennials can be inter-woven to provide more colour among the foliage. Argyranthemums have recently become very popular. Yellow varieties, such as 'Jamaica Primrose' and *A. maderense*, combine well with blue agapanthus, felicia or deep blue *Commelina coelestis*. Pink varieties, such as 'Vancouver' and 'Mary Wootton', look well with *Verbena* 'Sissinghurst' – or the taller *Verbena bonariensis*.

Arctotis, with its bright, daisy-like flowers, gazanias and osteospermums are all good plants for the front of a border. Another useful plant for the front is *Fascicularia bicolor*. It is a low-growing plant and in the autumn the leaves acquire vivid red splashes surrounding an ice-blue rosette of flowers.

Kniphofias – red hot pokers – are suitable plants to fill in corners of borders. *Kniphofia caulescens* and *K. northiae* both have very good foliage in addition to their attractive flowers.

Dahlias and salvias are very useful to extend the flowering season. *Salvia confertiflora* is a tall, attractive plant which bears spikes of red flowers. *S. leucantha* has purple flower spikes and the blue flowers of *S. patens* combine well with *Bidens aurea*. *Dahlia* 'Bishop of Llandaff', with its bronze foliage and brilliant red flowers, looks well against the silver plumes of Pampas Grass *Cortaderia selloana* 'Pumila' and the golden foliage of *Fuchsia* 'Genii'. *F.* 'Thalia' is another variety whose flowers contrast well with its dark red foliage. (*See also* DEALING WITH DAHLIAS, *p.106*.)

By using a selection of the plants mentioned a really colourful and exotic border can be achieved.

TIPS

1. Make some bamboo wigwams. Insert 3–4 canes into the ground in a circle. Tie them together at the top to form a wigwam shape. Plant some unusual tender climbers, such as *Rhodochiton volubilis* or *Maurandya erubescens*, to cover the wigwam.

2. Many plants mentioned here are not hardy and cuttings should be taken in autumn, or the plants taken inside before the winter frosts arrive.

OCTOBER
TO
DECEMBER

MAKING AND MAINTAINING A KNOT GARDEN

Valerie Hole, Head Gardener

ANTONY · TORPOINT · CORNWALL

Humphry Repton produced one of his first Red Books for this eighteenth-century landscape setting where sweeping lawns are edged with clipped yew hedges. A National Collection of Daylilies is based at Antony and there is a colourful summer display in the sheltered flower garden. The knot garden here uses box and germander.

The idea of the knot garden, which dates back to the fifteenth century, consists of a geometric pattern of dwarf hedges, often within a square. It may follow a heraldic design or the pattern of a knot, from which it gets its name. It is best to plan a knot garden symmetrically, on a level site which receives even light and which can be viewed from above.

Designing the plan

Make a plan on graph paper, then create a grid on the ground and transfer the design. Interlacing two different plants, giving precedence first to one then the other, gives the effect of threads running through a knot. Do not make it too complicated – remember you have to maintain it. If you are planting beds or grass between your hedges, allow space for maintenance.

Coloured gravels or earths may be better. Be meticulous – errors show. Create circles using a cane and string like a compass. Curves give more leeway – their shape can vary a little as they mature. Straight lines and right angles must be accurate. Mark out your area using sand, lines, canes or tape to show the whole design, then have a really good look at it before you proceed. It is best to get it right at this stage.

Plants to choose

Plants used in Tudor and Stuart knot gardens included marjoram (*Origanum vulgare*), rue (*Ruta graveolens*), thyme (*Thymus vulgaris*), Cotton Lavender (*Santolina chamaecyparissus*) and Hyssop (*Hyssopus officinalis*). Germander (*Teucrium × lucidrys T. chamaedrys* of gardens) and Dwarf Box (*Buxus sempervirens* 'Suffruticosa') are particularly good knot garden plants.

Cultivation

As with all permanent planting the ground should be well-cultivated. It is possible, however, to plant in either October/November or March. Space plants 3–4in/7.5–10cm apart. Do not have the width between hedges so precise that an inch or two of growth will spoil the whole effect. Keep some plants in reserve in case of losses.

Allow hedge plants to settle before you consider sowing grass or in-filling with plants. Avoid damage to the roots when you do plant around them. These plants are already stressed by growing in a quite unnatural manner. Keep weed free and protect from pests – hurdling the hedges can be a great joy for children and dogs.

Trimming

Once established the hedges may require trimming 2–4 times a year, depending on the plants and the season. Ideally they should be trimmed in August/September in order to achieve a little growth before winter. Avoid cutting into old wood, although all hedges gradually expand and may have to be cut back hard occasionally to keep the correct scale. A trim after the first flush of growth in spring gives a tidy appearance for the summer. Another may be required later.

If the knot garden is set in grass, the edges should be well-kept. They can then be used as a guide when using a hedge trimmer or shears. It is extremely difficult to maintain correct lines and height by eye, therefore straight edges and templates may be helpful.

Nutrition

Your knot garden must be fed in order to keep it healthy. Whenever you mow or prune you are removing nutrients and the capacity for nutrition. A slow-release fertiliser is advisable and a tidy mulch of well-rotted compost around the base of the hedges feeds the plants, retains moisture and restricts weeds. Within 18 months you should have a recognisable knot garden and within 3–5 years it will look as if it has been there for ever.

TIP

Gravel has a nasty habit of getting on to grass. It is difficult to remove with a moss rake, but turn the rake head over and you can sweep the gravel easily back on to the paths.

AUTUMN WORK IN THE HERBACEOUS BORDER

Robin Allan, Head Gardener

HARDWICK HALL · DOE LEA · CHESTERFIELD · DERBYSHIRE

Although little remains of Bess of Hardwick's late sixteenth-century garden, the Elizabethan spirit is maintained in the orchards, nuttery and herb garden. The borders in the west court were originally laid out in the 1830s. They are spectacular in late summer and autumn.

Autumn, as the dictionary defines it, is the season of incipient decay. The blaze of summer colour may linger in the memory but gaps will be appearing in our herbaceous borders where *Nepeta*, *Kniphofia*, *Rheum* and *Geranium* are getting tatty. It can be a difficult time to keep the borders looking good. We can leave the dried flower heads of some plants, eg *Salvia × superba*, as they are attractive even though they look parched.

Late blooms

Tender in-fill plants, like dahlias, *Cosmos atrosanguineus* and *Bidens ferulifolia*, are at their best in early autumn. The semi-hardy penstemons are still flowering, 'Garnet' being the hardiest. Tall blue spikes of *Aconitum* and the second flowering of delphiniums delay the thought of imminent frosts. It is frequently the first frost that signals that the time has come to tidy the borders by cutting all growth down to 3–6in/7.5–15cm from soil level.

Clearing away

It is important to clear away the cut herbage as it not only removes the possibility of pest and disease build-up, but reduces the amount of rotting organic matter on the soil surface, a favoured habitat of slugs. November to January is a good time for putting out slug pellets as hedgehogs hibernate; in fact you may well find their nests among the borders – great piles of dead vegetation, generally well-positioned between the plants. We always seem to have a nest amongst the *Hemerocallis*, the leaves of which become wet and soggy in the autumn. Remember slugs do not hibernate and in spring are frequently the cause of many a plant failure.

Marking the spot

When cutting down, remove all pea sticks and canes, saving only the latter for the following year. The positions of plants that were particularly small, choice or which die down completely with no surface evidence in the spring should be marked. Identify these areas with a few twigs or even canes as it is very easy to forget exactly where a particular favourite grew.

How to divide

The best way to divide herbaceous plants is to place two forks back-to-back, stab through the middle of the clump and lever the forks against each other. Always select the young growth on the outside of the clump for replanting and discard the old central core.

When to divide

Most herbaceous plants need to be lifted and divided every 3–5 years. This is a good time to dig in organic matter, especially if the soil is light, sandy, or just plain hungry – indicated by the very rapid disappearance of the organic matter. If you garden on heavy soil, then it is best to dig and divide in September while the soil is not too wet and there is still some heat in it to allow young roots to grow and become established before winter sets in. Those who garden on light soils can leave this task till spring when the ground is warming up again.

Plants like *Eryngium* need to be divided in the autumn; others like asters prefer to be propagated in March. It is worth doing a bit of homework, and if you have plenty of plant material, experiment for yourself – always the best way to learn.

Mulching

Peonies and hostas do not require frequent digging and dividing and in fact resent being disturbed; however an annual layer of mulch is very beneficial. *Agapanthus* like similar treatment and the layer of mulch helps to protect the young leaves from the early spring frosts.

TIP

With the borders put to bed there is little more to do till spring comes round. Spend the winter evenings browsing through books and nursery catalogues to find a particular plant that has the right height, colour and flowering season, will tolerate your soil and climate and fill the odd gap or even replace a poor performer.

PLANTING CONIFERS

David Masters, Head Gardener

NYMANS GARDEN · HANDCROSS · WEST SUSSEX

Famous for its collection of rare plants, this 30-acre Sussex Weald garden was created by the Messel family over three generations from 1890 to provide spectacular seasonal displays at all times of the year. The pinetum was replanted after the devastation of the 1987 storm.

October is a good time for planting conifers, assuming the weather is seasonal, the soil still warm from the summer sun and moistened by the early autumn rain.

Buying the right plant
First, choose your plant. The variety will depend on available space and personal preference regarding ultimate size, shape, colour of foliage and so on. Whatever your choice, it is important to purchase a healthy plant which looks as though it is enthusiastic about life.

Check the root system
Conifers can generally be purchased either in containers or 'bare rooted'. The former may be planted at any time of year provided

irrigation is possible. The latter, which are normally lifted from the nursery row and have their roots wrapped in hessian, are best planted in October. Whichever you buy, ensure that the root system is healthy and of sufficient size to support the amount of plant above ground. Knock container-grown plants out of their pots before purchase to ensure that they are not 'pot bound'. The roots should just fill the pot and not be circling around the inside looking for a way out.

Preparing the hole

When planting always dig a hole much wider than you think is necessary, at least twice the diameter of the root ball. If planting in a lawn, 3.2ft/1m across is about right for a tree that is going to grow taller than you. Cut a circle in the grass (circles look more natural than rectangles) and put the turf to one side. Then excavate the hole to a spade's depth, putting the soil to one side. The bottom of the hole should then be forked over to break up any compaction and the turf that you have lifted chopped up and incorporated into this. If your soil is poor, then organic matter, such as leaf-mould or garden compost, can be added. Then step into the hole and firm the soil. This will stop any settlement of the soil in the months following planting.

Planting

The plant can now be offered up to the planting hole to check its depth relative to the surrounding area. Place a bamboo or other straight edge across the hole and check that the top of the roof ball is level with or slightly (about 1in/2.5cm) above the rim of the hole. Conifers, in common with most plants, hate to be planted too deep. The stem of the tree is designed to live above ground, not below it. After adjusting the depth, you can start to backfill the hole around the root ball with the soil you put to one side. This too can be plumped up with organic matter before backfilling. Replace the soil, a little at a time, firming it around the root with your foot as you go, until the soil is level with the top of the hole, ensuring that the top of the root ball is still just visible.

Care and attention

Watering should not be necessary if conditions are right and fertilisers are not generally needed until 18 months after planting. If your plant had the correct sized root ball for its height staking shouldn't be required, although in windy positions a short, sturdy bamboo stake tied loosely to the stem will help to stop the root ball moving. The top of the plant should be allowed to move in the wind as this helps to build a strong stem. The stake should be removed a year after planting.

A circular mat of black polythene, slightly smaller than the planting hole, can be put around the base of the plant. This has two beneficial effects. It completely stops the growth of weeds, which not only look unsightly but also compete for nutrients, and prevents evaporation of soil moisture. However, polythene is not pretty and a mulch of bark, compost or gravel will put the finishing touch to the job.

TIP

When buying a new conifer plant look at the top of the compost in the pot. If it is covered in annual weeds or moss then it has been around too long.

LAWN RENOVATION

Philip Cotton, Head Gardener

CLIVEDEN · TAPLOW · MAIDENHEAD · BERKSHIRE

A large landscape, Cliveden has a sequence of historical garden styles from early eighteenth-century avenues and rides by Charles Bridgeman to herbaceous borders in the Gertrude Jekyll style, an oriental water garden made in 1900 to a glade garden designed by Geoffrey Jellicoe in 1959.

By this time of year, lawns have suffered the stress of the whole season, so the grass plants need help to restore themselves to good condition for next year.

Dealing with severe damage

The greatest problem for a lawn which has suffered drought during the summer, especially on free-draining poor soil, is having been trampled by many feet. This is a disaster if the carefully mown lawn is a major element of an important design. The problem is even worse if the soil structure beneath the drying grass has been changed by a fungus that actually repels water, making irrigation impossible. Only the application of a wetting agent will solve this problem. Really bad areas will then require re-seeding.

Operations required

(1) Remove thatch (dead grass etc, lying on soil surface), with a spring tine rake or scarifier.

(2) Aerate to encourage root action and break compaction with a fork or machine. (A hollow-core tine type which removes a soil plug is best for compacted lawns.)

(3) Cultivate areas for re-seeding with a rake or scarifier. Re-seeding requires a tilth of loose soil for germination.

(4) Feed the lawn a liquid (seaweed) fertiliser and wetting agent combined, applied by watering can or sprayer. Autumn feed is low in nitrogen but high in phosphate and potash to assist root development and 'hard' foliage for winter.

(5) Overseed by scattering on prepared areas either by hand or with a distributor.

Sophisticated machines that scarify, sweep, apply powder or mini-crumb fertiliser and distribute seed in one operation can be hired for large areas, but not for small lawns. The satisfaction gained from doing the job well by hand brings its own reward!

Springtime tasks

When spring comes, lawns which have not suffered so badly still benefit from:

(1) Scarifying, to open up the surface, letting in air and water.

(2) Aerating, again to let in air, water and fertiliser, while breaking compaction.

(3) Spring feeding which has more nitrogen in proportion to phosphate and potash, to encourage growth and improve lawn colour. However, do not apply the feed for four days after mowing or 'burning' may occur.

Weed control

Excessive weeds in a lawn can be controlled by selective weed killers, applied in still weather with no rain imminent. A sprayer or a watering can with 'dribble bar' are used. An alternative is to use combined fertilisers and weed killers in powder form; a ferrous sulphate moss killer is also added to some proprietary formulations. The time for moss control is either September or March onwards. However, environmental concerns now impose strict controls on the use of chemicals throughout horticulture.

Take great care with application and abide strictly by the instructions on the labels. By far the best way of discouraging moss, weeds and diseases that spoil lawns is to have healthy, vigorous grass plants of the correct species growing in good condition.

TIP
Most lawns have some weeds (and some of us like a few daisies and buttercups anyway). If you don't want the same weeds on the rose beds, resist the temptation to mulch them with the fresh lawn mowings. Far better to empty the grass box on to the compost heap, and later use the compost as a mulch!

COMPOST MAKING

Malcolm Simms, Assistant Head Gardener

ROWALLANE GARDEN · SAINTFIELD · BALLYNAHINCH · CO. DOWN

The delightfully natural garden at Rowallane was planned by Hugh Armytage Moore who inherited the property in 1903. He had a special eye for plants and collected them, especially those from the Far East. The lovely spring display is followed by rhododendrons and azaleas and there is an outstanding rock garden. There are also rare specimens for the collector to admire.

Obviously our compost making at Rowallane is done on a large scale, but the method can still be used in smaller gardens and the quantities proportionately reduced.

Where to build

We have an area set aside for compost making where we assemble piles of wood chips, soil, leaf-mould, farmyard manure, mushroom compost, stones and gravel. There is also a fire known as the 'dump'. Perhaps we should call it the compost-making factory. The area has a hard surface underneath, made up from broken stones. On each side there are trees to shelter and screen the area and overhang the compost heaps, providing some shade.

Our compost heaps are free-standing, but compost 'heaps' can also be made by sinking them in holes in the ground, which has the advantage of keeping the heat in. The ground at the base of the heap is left uncovered, enabling micro-organisms to make their way into the compost. Stalks and stems of plants that take a long time to decompose are placed at the base of the heap to improve drainage.

135

The use of weeds

On top of the well-drained base, generous layers of green plant matter are placed. These consist of weeds, leaves and stems from the garden. Avoid pernicious weeds, eg convolvulus, whose seeds or roots will grow even after composting, and keep them separate from the material to be composted. Nor do we use rose leaves, in case of blackspot, or the clippings of a lawn which has just been treated with herbicide.

Most weeds make better compost if they are gathered before they start to seed as they have more foliage at this stage.

Using herbage

At Rowallane at the end of September we cut our wildflower meadows. This means we have a lot of similar material to compost at the same time. We add it to our compost heap in layers about 2ft/60cm thick. Next we add a 2–3in/5–8cm layer of partly rotted manure, followed by another layer of wildflower herbage. After this herbage layer, we put on a 2in/5cm layer of partly rotted wood chips, then back to a layer of wildflower herbage, followed by manure and so on. When all the wildflower herbage and layers are on, the heap will stand about 8–9ft/2.4–2.7m high. Long before this, of course, we have been using a tractor with a front loader to add the layers. We add a final top layer of manure and wood chips to cap the heap and then start a new pile, using the stems and stalks of herbaceous plants to make the base.

When putting the wildflower herbage on, it is best to cut and place it directly on the heap while it is still green and has nitrogen in it, because this is helpful to the microbial decomposition process. If the wildflower herbage is allowed to turn into hay, it will be mostly carbon and will be slow to decompose. This will lower the nitrogen in the compost rather than increase it. Some years our wildflower herbage does end up like this, so then we apply sulphate of ammonia to the layers to supply nitrogen and accelerate decomposition.

Manure

We add manure which contains live humus to start the process of decomposition. The bacteria in the manure reproduce quickly so that when the compost is used in a bed or border, it will add to the range of living things already in the soil.

Water with care

After the heap is built it is left to decompose. It will need to be watered only if it gets too dry. If it gets too wet and becomes sour it will need to be turned but this does not usually happen. After about five or six months we turn our heap and leave it again. One year we put a heap through a soil shredder, making it finer and suitable for use in our rock garden as a mulch. On other areas it does not need this extra breaking down.

We have thought of putting the material for the compost heap through a machine to break it up before it goes on the heap, but I now think this may be harmful as the heap then becomes soggy if it gets too wet. The heap needs air for the beneficial micro-organisms to do their work and keeping the material coarse will help to keep the air in, preventing it from going sour.

It may seem strange but the best way to help the life of the soil is to give it the remains of living plants – your compost.

TIP

Look after the bacteria and they will look after the compost. To meet the needs of bacteria:

1. keep the heat in;

2. keep excessive water out;

3. ensure the right balance between carbon and nitrogen;

4. add some soil or farmyard manure to mop up water and harmful gases. The manure also provides a dose of helpful bacteria which will reproduce quickly.

PRUNING TREES

Peter Borlase, retired Head Gardener

LANHYDROCK · BODMIN · CORNWALL

Lanhydrock has over 30 acres of gardens, which include formal gardens to the front of the late Victorian house, and beyond a more informal area on steep slopes with large magnolias, rhododendrons and camellias.

Although pruning is a purely artificial operation, it is based on one of nature's processes. In the wild, superfluous branches die back and often every part of the plant has to fight for a place amongst its fellows. In the garden this is not so. The gardener's aim is to provide each plant with conditions that will enable it to develop the qualities he requires, and by removing adverse influences enable the plant to devote its whole energy to these ends.

Objectives

Pruning is performed either to reduce or restrict a tree or shrub to some desired size or shape, to regulate the quality and quantity of the flowers or fruit, or to improve the health and increase the vitality of old and sickly trees. The objectives are simple and self-evident, yet it is a fact that of all the horticultural arts pruning is the one most misapplied and misunderstood, often being done without regard to the habits of plants or their times of flowering. (*See also* PRUNING AND TRAINING CLIMBERS, *p.19*, PRUNING SHRUBS, *p.23*, PRUNING ROSES, *p.32*.)

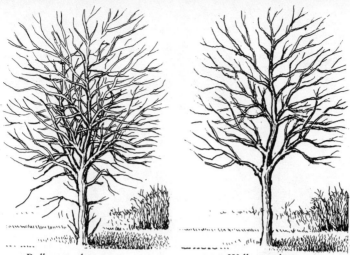

FIG.1 *Badly-pruned tree.*　　　　　FIG.2 *Well-pruned tree.*

Best practice

Pruning is a gardening process which requires careful thought and intelligence, and an acquaintance with the nature of the plant. Good pruning can immensely improve the beauty or usefulness of a plant, but it is infinitely better to leave alone rather than prune badly. It is said that pruning should be done with finger and thumb, by pinching out superfluous or objectionable growths. Though a great deal can be done in this way, the amount of time and attention such a method would entail in a large garden is beyond our reach in this day and age.

To prune or not to prune?

There are those who hold that no tree or shrub should ever be touched with a knife or saw on the assumption that, if left alone, every plant will attain a true beauty that human skill cannot hope to match. In our gardens, however, this philosophy cannot be applied as we grow trees and shrubs from all over the world; hundreds of species, which in their natural state grow in a variety of conditions from mountain to plain, forest or valley. We bring them together in one place where conditions, climate, soil and rainfall are fairly uniform. Without the gardener's intervention the differing and unequal growth of all these plants would, in time, create a very untidy impression.

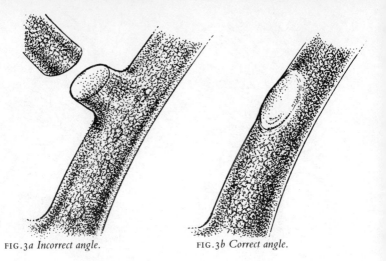

FIG. 3a *Incorrect angle.*   FIG. 3b *Correct angle.*

When to prune?

The time to prune a large-growing tree is when it is young, for then it is comparatively easy to correct any deformities. It is also less stressful to a deciduous tree to prune when it has no leaves and its shape is more clearly defined. It should be borne in mind that whilst pruning enables the gardener to promote the development of the wood where it is most needed (and to prevent the formation of useless or unsightly branches), the growth of all woody plants is directly dependent on the amount of leaf surface. A weak growth unable to support itself may result from the over hasty removal of lower branches or too severe pruning, so one has to be very careful to prune away just the correct amount.

TIP

Take care to angle the cut correctly when pruning. An incorrect angle (*fig.3a*) can cause fungoid disease. The correct angle (*fig.3b*) will heal over much more quickly and prevent subsequent damage to the tree or shrub.

IVIES
A CELEBRATION

Glyn Smith, Head Gardener

ERDDIG · NR WREXHAM · CLWYD

A bird's-eye view of Erddig, engraved in 1740, enabled the Trust to restore the formal eighteenth-century layout. The garden is divided into sections by symmetrical walks, hedges, water and lawns. In front of the house there is a Victorian bedded parterre and young pleached limes flank the central walk.

> The Holly and the Ivy
> When they are both full grown
> Of all the trees that are in the wood
> The Holly bears the crown.

Poor old ivy, the only time it gets a mention is at the beginning and end of the carol when it makes us think of winter. We also associate it with death and dank Victorian cemeteries, although we are meant to see this plant as a symbol of life and celebration.

The meaning of ivy

Alexander the Great's victorious army, on its return from India, was said to be crowned with wreaths of rare ivy. From Roman times, bunches of ivy called 'Alestakes' were hung outside inns, signifying that new ale or wine was ready for sale. This practice gave rise to the saying 'A good wine needs no bush'. The Victorians used ivy in wedding bouquets to symbolise faithfulness, suggested by the way it clings, supports and lasts for such a long time.

Ivy as a houseplant

Ivy was possibly the favourite Victorian houseplant, used as decoration, trained around windows and doorways, or as permanent planting around troughs and seats. Other plants would be added to give flower colour according to the season. Today we tend to grow ivy as a houseplant in its own right; almost everyone has had an ivy as a houseplant at some time and it is often planted out in the garden when it grows too large. Most of the houseplant ivies are slow growing and, although just as hardy as their more vigorous brothers and sisters, may change slightly in appearance once they start climbing up a wall or rooting along the ground.

Ivy in the garden

The uses of ivy in the garden are endless – it covers walls, climbs up tree trunks or over stumps, creeps as ground cover under trees, wanders down steep banks or over beds, is trained up walls, over arches, along fences or is used as a 'fedge' (a clipped hedge of ivy initially supported by or hiding a fence). It is also used in tubs or pots, window boxes and hanging baskets. Some varieties are suitable for rock gardens and bottle gardens and most can be trained over wires or moss-filled shapes as topiary. Trailing standards are produced by tying ivy up to canes then pinching out the tips to make a cascade.

As well as its juvenile, climbing stage, ivy also has a shrubby adult stage when it flowers. The Victorians used to propagate these 'ivy trees' to use as free-standing bushes in bedding schemes in winter. They often had berries after flowering, usually grey-black, or orange in the case of Poet's Ivy, and could also be grafted and trained rather like standard roses.

Cultivars

There are over 3,000 known cultivars. Most nurseries stock only a few of the best known, although good selections can be found in the specialist nurseries. At Erddig we have around 90 cultivars on display, and we add more each year. About 150–200 should give us a comprehensive selection of the best leaf shapes, variegations and species that can be grown.

Does ivy damage buildings?

The tiny adventitious roots that grow from the stems of ivies, attaching them to walls and fences, do not cause damage. After a season or so these die, although they continue to fix the plant to its support. In time the plant can attain such a size that these rootlets cannot support the weight and the ivy will peel off, usually without causing any damage. Sometimes, soft mortar is pulled away and some re-pointing may be required.

As long as walls and pointing are in good order, the ivies are regularly clipped and the shoots kept away from large cracks, drainpipes, windows, wires, gutters and slates, there should be little cause for worry and the ivy can even help to insulate the house, keeping it warm and dry.

As for roots damaging foundations – again, this should not be a problem. However, there is a story that at Magdalen College, Oxford, the roots of an ivy found their way to the cellar and into a bottle of vintage port which was consumed, leaving only a bottleful of roots. The dons must have found this a very dry port indeed!

TIP

Traditional topiary of box or yew can take many years to grow, and we can become bored waiting for it to mature. More instant topiary can be achieved by training ivy over wire frames or planting it into moss-filled chicken-wire shapes. The varied colour and leaf shapes of ivy also allow for more imaginative designs than the traditional dark green of box or yew topiary.

PLANTING AND ESTABLISHING TREES

Trevor Seddon, Head Gardener

PETWORTH PARK AND GARDENS · WEST SUSSEX

Petworth's 650-acre park, with its two lakes and herd of 1,000 deer, was landscaped by Capability Brown. He also designed the pleasure grounds which are notable for bulbs and wild flowers in spring, herbaceous borders in summer and late autumn colour. Since the 1987 storm, 32,000 trees have been planted at Petworth.

November is an ideal month to plant trees. They are dormant, temperatures are not too low and roots will be settled and ready to explore by spring. However, planting can be done successfully from November to March with bare root trees, provided the soil is not frozen or waterlogged. Pot-grown plants are designed for year-round planting subject to reasonable soil conditions.

Tree size

Originally, all trees grew from seed, suckers or layers and were never transplanted, so the nearer one can get to this ideal the better. Commercially grown trees are sometimes transplanted too close together in the nursery, causing thin drawn stems with side branches pruned away. If pot grown for several years they may have severely restricted roots set in spiral fashion. Buy small 1–3ft/30–90cm trees with sturdy stems, side branches intact and a good spreading root system if open grown.

Planting

For best results, remove the turf from a 3ft/0.9m circle. Dig out the soil to a depth of 1ft/30cm, loosen the base of the hole with a fork, place the inverted turf in the bottom. Make up a mixture of one-third well-rotted manure or compost and two-thirds removed soil. Place the tree in the hole with roots well spread out, teasing them out of the circle if pot grown. Plant to the depth indicated by the soil mark on the tree collar. Firm the soil with the ball of your foot (not with the heel). There is little advantage in adding extra fertiliser at this point; the compost should provide all that is necessary for most soil types.

Staking

If your tree is small with a good root system, staking is unnecessary and could cause damage. If the tree really will not stand in a wind unaided, use a short stake driven into the windward side of the excavated hole to protrude 1–3ft/30–90cm. The size of the stake will depend on tree height, crown size and stem diameter. All that it needs to do is to stop the roots being lifted out. Research now indicates what close observation should have told us anyway, that flexing and bending promotes stem thickening. Use a good strap with a distance piece. Remove stake and strap one season later in the spring, two years later if really necessary. However, you may have to restake at any time after serious gales.

Maintenance

Friendly competition may stimulate people but it is bad news for trees. Grass is the worst offender. Always keep it as far away from the stem of newly planted stock as aesthetically possible – 3ft/0.9m circle is the minimum. This can be achieved with good old traditional hoeing or forking, weed-free compost, leaves, bark, wood chippings or grass mowings laid no deeper than 9in/23cm. Or try the latest mulch matting, felt or other ground cover fabric – anything is better than grass.

Herbicides

Much as we hate them, they do achieve remarkable results and may be the only way to get rid of weeds when tending large numbers of trees. As yet, glyphosate, sold under various trade names, seems to have a clean bill of health and is apparently inactivated quickly in the soil. Don't get it on the bark or the leaves. Do read the labels carefully.

TIP

When do trees feed most hungrily? The spring flush demands most from the soil nutrients, so spray out the competition in late March to mid-April and again in June to encourage the later growth.

PLANTING, PRUNING AND TRAINING VINES

Brian Wilde, Gardener-in-Charge

CLUMBER PARK · WORKSOP · NOTTINGHAMSHIRE

At Clumber Park a cedar-lined walk connects the informal pleasure grounds to the walled kitchen garden where the magnificent vineries house not only grapes, figs and exotic plants but also a museum. Here is an exhibition of nineteenth-century kitchen gardening with tools, a potting shed, an apple store and a gardener's mess room.

December is an ideal month to plant a vine in your glasshouse. If you have a lean-to glasshouse, position the vine in the centre of the front wall. If the house has a span-roof, the centre of the end wall opposite the door is the best place. Do not forget that you have to allow the roots access to the outside.

Wiring

It is best to do this job before planting. Fix the horizontal support wires the full length of the glasshouse. They should be fixed firmly at each end and spaced about 18in/46cm apart and about 12in/30cm from the roof. Galvanised wire of $\frac{1}{16}$in/1.6mm gauge should be used for this purpose and jute fillis should be used to tie in the vine.

Preparing the spot

Dig a pit 3ft/0.9m square and 3ft/0.9m deep, inside your glasshouse. Place a 9in/23cm layer of brick rubble in the bottom of the hole and cover this with whole turves, grass side down, and refill with fibrous loam. Mix well together 2lb/0.9kg each of

147

bonemeal and hoof and horn meal. Add this evenly as you refill. Add 8oz/226g of lime separately.

Plant your vine in this mixture before mid-January. Cut back the stem to within 6–12in/15–30cm of its base and secure it to a cane. One vine will be ample to fill the average-sized glasshouse.

Pruning and training

During the first season in a lean-to glasshouse, when growth starts, select the strongest shoot and remove all others. Allow this shoot to develop as the main rod. Train this straight up the roof until it can grow no further. Stop it and remove all side shoots as they appear. In December cut right back to wall plate height (that is, to where the roof and wall of the glasshouse meet).

Second season

Allow two shoots only to develop off the main stem (one each side if possible). Train one of these each way along the wall plate wire, tie in carefully as they grow and stop them when they reach the ends of the glasshouse. Allow one vertical shoot to grow off each horizontal stem about 2ft/0.6m on each side of the main stem. Again, tie in as they grow, let them grow as far as they can and stop. In December, cut these rods back to a bud about 3ft/0.9m from the wall plate laterals. Then cut the wall plate laterals back to a bud about 4ft/1.2m from this vertical rod.

Third season

Allow wall plate laterals to grow from the bud to the end of the house and treat as the previous year. When the buds begin to grow, train in one more vertical rod on each side about 4ft/1.2m away from the first ones.

Treat the first vertical rod as follows. Allow it to grow from the bud then stop as before. On the previous year's growth (brown wood) allow the laterals to grow and tie them carefully to wires, stopping at the second or third leaf. Do not be greedy; allow only 4–5 bunches of grapes to grow this year. Stop the non-fruiting laterals at 18in/45cm and prune all these back to within 1–2 buds of the rod in December.

Subsequent seasons

Treat the vine in the same way until the glasshouse is fully furnished.

Span-roofed glasshouse

In a glasshouse with a span roof, train the main rod under the apex of the roof and other rods down the roof from this. Prune in the way already described.

Before new growth starts

One very important task remains to be done. When December pruning is completed, to ensure even shooting of the laterals in spring, the main rods should be lowered from the roof and placed in a downward sloping position for a few weeks before new shoots begin to grow. Tie back in the original places *immediately* new growth starts and *never* remove large shoots early in the season as they will bleed and damage the vine.

TIPS

1. Old molehills provide ideal material for refilling the hole in which you plant the vine.

2. Feed your vine three times at 6-week intervals from March with 6oz/170g of dried blood per dose sprinkled on and lightly forked in.

PATH MAKING

Robert James, Head Gardener

GLENDURGAN · HELFORD RIVER · MAWNAN SMITH · NR FALMOUTH
CORNWALL

Originally planted in the 1820s and 1830s by the prosperous owner of a local shipping company, Glendurgan has a fine collection of trees, rhododendrons, camellias, magnolias and delightful spring flowers. An unusual feature is the Holy Bank, planted with trees and shrubs with Biblical associations.

At Glendurgan the majority of our paths are steep, and we have problems with path erosion at junctions and tight corners on slopes, where our compact tractor chews up the surface making it rough, slippery and dangerous. We also face the problem of erosion from heavy rain, when water rushes down the paths scouring the surface.

Materials

We need a hard-wearing, grippy, permanent, natural surface with an element of drainage. It also needs to feel safe to the general public. The answer to these essential requirements is to construct paths from stone. Our natural stone is a thin, grey shale which has been used throughout the garden for path edging, and we have a good local supply.

Larger stone, of about twice the size of the surface stone, was needed for returning the edges of the banks. Some sort of structure had to separate the gravel path surface from the stone section and as drainage was a problem, we decided upon a pre-cast, weight-tested, polychannel gulley with a slatted cast-iron grid. These gullies come in 39in/1m lengths with 19½in/0.5m cast-iron gratings.

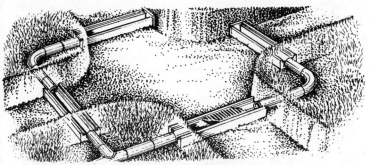

FIG.1 *Excavated trench with drainage gullies and pipes in place.*

Excavation of the site

Should you plan to carry out similar work, excavation of the site is the first step. Allow enough room for the larger stones to be cemented in on the sides and enough depth to allow some fine grade quarry stone to be added to the base. (We use $\frac{3}{4}$in to dust grade.) The excavation width must allow tractor and trailer room to turn corners as the trailer will go wider than the tractor.

Compaction

The next step involves compacting the excavated base of the path; add a good layer of the fine quarry grade dust, then compact the surface further.

Drainage channels

Place drainage channels at the end of the desired stone section across the path and cement in. Match the colour of the paths and stone with the appropriately coloured sand or dye the cement. These channels should link up with existing drains or into a soak-away.

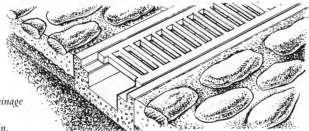

FIG.2 *Drainage channels cemented in.*

Side retaining stones

The side retaining stones can now be cemented into position. The stones can be placed flat along the edge, as in *fig. 3a*, or placed side-by-side, as in *fig. 3b*, which is stronger but uses more stones.

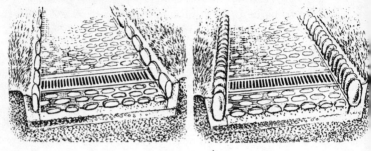

FIG. 3*a*   FIG. 3*b*

Placing the smaller stones

Once the edging stones and drainage channels have been left to set, the smaller stones can be added. Lay down a thick bed of cement in a strip across the path next to the drainage channel. Start pushing the smaller stones into this, on their edge. Repeat this with the next row, alternating them as if building a brick wall. The stones should be placed in the cement to three-quarters of their depth and the finished cement level should be the same as the drainage grid.

FIG. 4

As you progress towards the corners, start angling the stones. As the stones are being placed, stamp them level with a board laid on top. The tighter the stones are placed together the better the finished surface looks. (*fig. 4*)

As you progress, only do as much each day as you can clean off and leave to harden. Wash off excess cement using a soft brush and a watering can fitted with a rose to clean up the stone.

Finishing off

Once the surface has dried and hardened off, soil or turf can be placed on to the top of the edging stones. Once it has weathered a little it will be a hard-wearing surface that feels safe and grippy to walk on and tough enough for the tractor to drive over.

Maintenance

If a stone becomes loose, it may be necessary to re-cement it back in place. Path gravel and leaves can be blown or swept off as required.

TIP
When mixing cement, try to make the mixture fairly dry, although moist enough to allow the stones to be pushed into it.

USING PLANTS FROM NEW ZEALAND

Nigel Marshall, Head Gardener

MOUNT STEWART · NEWTOWNARDS · CO. DOWN

The collection of plants at Mount Stewart is unrivalled, largely due to the vision of Edith, wife of the 7th Marquess of Londonderry, who began to recreate the garden in 1921. Thanks to the soft mild climate, rhododendrons, exotic trees and many southern hemisphere plants are able to flourish here.

People who garden along the western seaboard of the British Isles benefit from the influence of the Gulf Stream. This produces a milder winter climate to that experienced on the eastern coast of Britain. Unfortunately most coastal areas are ravaged by salt-laden gales at intervals from September to April, which makes the selection of plants for the garden very difficult. Generally, plants with a maritime inheritance, whose forebears have adapted themselves to exposed coastal environments in other parts of the world, are most likely to thrive.

Why New Zealand?

The geography and climate of New Zealand, especially the South Island, can in some ways be compared to parts of the western side of the United Kingdom. Both are mountainous with long coastlines and are therefore exposed to constant gales. Frosts can occur in most areas of New Zealand although rarely in the sub-tropical North Island.

The flora of New Zealand is unique and diverse with over 80 per cent found nowhere else in the world. Most are evergreen, with thick, leathery foliage of varying shapes and sizes. It is an interesting fact that the majority of New Zealand plants produce white flowers.

Hardwood trees

In the bleakest coastal exposures, where native British hardwood trees such as sycamore or ash struggle to survive, several New Zealand plants are quite at home. The toughest of these must be *Brachyglottis rotundifolia* (syn. *Senecio rotundifolius*), which can be expected to reach at least 8ft/2.4m high, and as much across, in about ten years. Its large round leaves, polished green above, are as tough as leather. Other *Brachyglottis*, such as *B. buchananii*, *B. greyi*, *B.* 'Sunshine' and *B. monroi*, are equally happy but do not grow as large.

Olearias

The daisy bushes or olearias comprise roughly 130 species, some 30 of them native to New Zealand. No other genus has more to offer maritime gardens. For severe exposure *O. traversii* × *O. macrodonta* 'Major' and *O. paniculata* (syn. *O. forsteri*), are amongst the front runners. Others, such as *O.* 'Henry Travers' (syn. *O. semidentata*), *O. phlogopappa* (syn. *O. gunniana*), *O. ramulosa*, *O. stellulata* (syn. *O. scilloniensis*) and *O. floribunda*, are all exceptional garden plants but require more sheltered positions.

Phormiums

Phormiums, or New Zealand flax, are very imposing architectural plants with tough, evergreen, sword-like leaves. They will stand a lot of severe exposure and if planted in association with cordylines (cabbage palms) produce a striking sub-tropical effect in gardens. There are several new hybrid phormiums on the market with foliage of varying reds, pinks, bronzes and creams. Mount Stewart holds the National Collection of Phormiums.

Best for butterflies

Hebes are evergreen shrubs varying in size from dwarfs 6–9in/15–22cm high to others reaching 8–10ft/2.5–3m. This family contains over 80 species and hybrids with varying leaf shapes and sizes. Some are grown mainly for foliage. The best flowering species and hybrids produce short spikes of flowers from mid- to late summer in shades of blue, pink, white and red – all much loved by butterflies.

More shrubs

Other evergreen shrubs are pittosporums, of which there are almost 30 New Zealand species, and griselinias. Recently hybridists have provided us with several variegated and coloured leaved forms of pittosporum. Among the tea trees (*Leptospermum*) are several suitable for coastal gardens. Eventually reaching some 10–15ft/3–4m in height, they bear masses of hawthorn-like flowers of white, shades of pink, or red in late May to June. They are easily raised from seed.

Maintenance

The key to success with these subjects is to plant them when small. If left in pots for a few years to grow on, the root system will become distorted and they will never become properly established in any exposed position.

TIP

For the first few years after planting, reduce the top growth of your plants by about a third every year to stop them becoming top heavy.

Index